Crapshoot Investing:

How Tech-Savvy Traders and Clueless Regulators Turned the Stock Market into a Casino

Jim McTague

Vice President, Publisher Tim Moore

Associate Publisher and Director of Marketing Amy Neidlinger

Executive Editor Jim Boyd

Editorial Assistant Pamela Boland

Development Editor Russ Hall

Operations Manager Gina Kanouse

Senior Marketing Manager Julie Phifer

Publicity Manager Laura Czaja

Assistant Marketing Manager Megan Colvin

Cover Designer Chuti Prasertsith

Managing Editor Kristy Hart

Project Editor Anne Goebel

Copy Editor Gill Editorial Services

Proofreader Water Crest Publishing

Senior Indexer Cheryl Lenser

Senior Compositor Gloria Schurick

Manufacturing Buyer Dan Uhrig

FT Press offers excellent discounts on this book when ordered in quantity for bulk purchases or special sales. For more information, please contact U.S. Corporate and Government Sales, 1-800-382-3419, corpsales@pearsontechgroup.com. For sales outside the U.S., please contact International Sales at international@pearson.com.

First Printing March 2011

Pearson Education LTD.
Pearson Education Australia PTY, Limited.
Pearson Education Singapore, Pte. Ltd.
Pearson Education Asia, Ltd.
Pearson Education Canada, Ltd.
Pearson Educatión de Mexico, S.A. de C.V.
Pearson Education—Japan
Pearson Education Malaysia, Pte. Ltd.

Library of Congress Cataloging-in-Publication Data:

McTague, Jim, 1949-
  Crapshoot investing : how tech-savvy traders and clueless regulators turned the stock market into a casino / Jim McTague.
    p. cm.
  ISBN 978-0-13-259968-9 (hardback : alk. paper)
  1. Investment analysis—United States. 2. Stock exchanges—Law and legislation—United States. 3. Electronic trading of securities. 4. Stocks—Law and legislation—United States. 5. Capital market—United States. I. Title.
  HG4529.M397 2011
  332.64'273—dc22

                         2010051301

ISBN-10: 0-13-259968-6
ISBN-13: 978-0-13-259968-9

To my wife, Rachel, for her understanding, help, and encouragement.

Contents

Acknowledgments

I want to thank my most memorable college professor and lifelong friend, Francis Burch, S.J., a brilliant scholar and author who encouraged me to become a columnist and an author.

This book was produced under a tight deadline to bring very important information to the attention of the investing public. I would not have been able to tackle the project without the encouragement of my colleagues at Barron's: Editor and President Edwin Finn; Managing Editor Richard Rescigno; and Assistant Managing Editor Phil Roosevelt. I also owe thanks to my officemate Tom Donlan, our editorialist and the author of several books, for his suggestions, especially those regarding Harvey Houtkin.

Chris Anderson, one of the smartest men on Wall Street, provided me with insights about the changing nature of the equities market. Ken Safian, another Wall Street legend, offered invaluable insights about high-frequency trading. Jamie Selway of Investment Technology Group LLC shared insights on market structure.

Will Ackworth of the Futures Industry Association was exceedingly generous in sharing his knowledge about the history of the commodities markets. Wayne Lee of NASDAQ, Ray Pellecchia of the NYSE Euronext, John Heine of the Securities and Exchange Commission, and Dan Chicoine of TD Ameritrade were especially helpful in connecting with market experts.

I also want to thank the many lawyers, regulators, and traders who spoke to me about market structure and high-frequency trading on deep background.

Finally, I offer special thanks to my daughter Alex, a patent litigator, and Bob Schewd of WilmerHale, a brilliant literary contract attorney, for assisting me in my negotiations with the publisher.

About the Author

Jim McTague has been Washington Editor of *Barron's Magazine* since 1994—a post that gives him privileged access to key players in Washington and on Wall Street. A credentialed White House and Capitol Hill correspondent, he's covered every administration since the first President Bush. McTague has appeared on NBC, CNN, CNBC, MSNBC, FOX, and is a frequent guest on FOX Business News. His extensive analysis of the underground economy in 2005 exploded the myth that illegal aliens were a small percentage of the U.S. population, triggering today's border security debate. McTague holds an MA in English from Pennsylvania State University and a BS in English from St. Joseph's University in Philadelphia.

Introduction

The stock market has changed radically since 2005, yet few persons realized the greatness of the seismic shift until May 6, 2010, when the major averages collapsed over the course of 10 minutes. The public suddenly realized that a venue designed to efficiently move capital from investors to the most promising enterprises had become as risky as a Las Vegas casino. This book is the story of well-intentioned but disastrously wrong-headed decisions by Congress and securities regulators that resulted in the destruction of a great American institution and possible long-lasting damage to the entire U.S. economy. Fixing this mess is without a doubt the most important challenge for U.S. policy makers in the years ahead, yet few of them understand this. They are still looking backward at the credit crisis of 2007 to 2008 and fail to see the bigger threat that is right before their eyes.

Just prior to May 6 during the first quarter of 2010, the all-clear siren sounded for shell-shocked Wall Street investors. All seemed well with the stock market. The major stock indexes, which had hit 12-year lows in March 2009 in the midst of the turbulent Great Recession, miraculously recovered by 74% the same month a year later. Investors once again were able to look at the returns in their retirement accounts without becoming physically ill. Confidence in the stock market, which had been badly shaken during the market meltdown of the previous two years, began to strengthen. In April 2010, retail investors began shifting money from safe havens like gold, commodities, and treasury bonds into equities and equity mutual funds, which was good news for cash-starved American enterprises.

Investors were understandably cautious—nervous as cats, actually—owing to what they had been through. And the stock market, despite its remarkable rebound, remained a frightening place. It was prone to jolting aftershocks in the form of wild, inexplicable, intraday price swings that saw the Dow Jones Industrial Average (DJIA) rising and falling by 100 or more points in a matter of hours. Prior to 2008, this sort of dramatic, volatile, intra-day shifting was rare. Often it took months for the DJIA to move 100 points, not half a day. Investors had grown accustomed over the years to parking their savings in the stock market for the long haul in the expectation of fairly predictable returns, not wild, hourly reversals of fortune. Since 2008, however, the market had become radically unstable, with 15 of the 20 largest intra-day price swings in the history of the DJIA having occurred in 2008.[1] Heightened volatility seemed to be a new normal. Volatility as measured by the Chicago Board of Options Exchange SPX Volatility Index or the VIX had been highly elevated in both 2008 and 2009.[2]

An intraday move of 3% in the Standard & Poor's (S&P) 500 is considered unusually large. According to Birinyi Associates, a stock market research group, there were 42 days with 3% moves in 2008 compared to 1 day in 2007 and 0 days from 2004 through 2006 (see Figure I.1). Moves of 2% are significant. There were 149 2% days during the 1990s and nearly as many—131 from 2000 through 2006—explained in part by the devastating 9-11 attacks. The Great Recession beginning in 2007 eclipsed that trying period, with 156 days of 2% moves (see Figure I.2).

The market's intraday swings were particularly unnerving during the 146 trading days between October 1, 2008 and March 31, 2009.[3] Retail investors typically invest first thing in the morning, at the market opening. On these wild days, their newly purchased shares often dropped significantly in value by the time the market closed at 4 p.m. EST. Consequently, equity investors began to lose that old-time, buy-and-hold religion and became risk adverse to the extreme. No item of bad news was ignored; no piece of good news was accepted uncritically. No new money was flowing into the stock market, either.

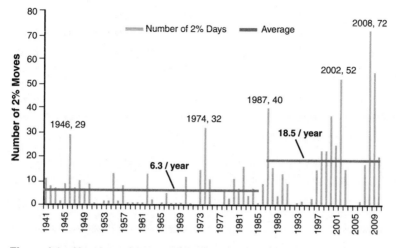

Figure I.1   Number of 2% +– Market Moves per Year.

Source: Birinyi Associates

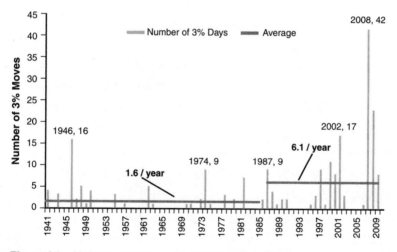

Figure I.2   Number of 3% +– Market Moves per Year.

Source: Birinyi Associates

"It's a *show me* market," said Robert Doll, the chief equity strate-gist at BlackRock Inc. "Fresh in everybody's mind is the carnage of late 2008 and 2009. Therefore, their mentality is to sell first and ask questions later."[4]

By early 2010, investors were not only exhausted, they were depleted. Most had seen their nest eggs reduced from 30% to 50% in

2007 and 2008. None but those who had lived through the Great Depression had ever experienced anything quite so frightening. Certainly, there had been tough times in the past, with recessions of 16-months duration in both the 1970s and 1980s. But equities since 1983 generally had been appreciating. Year after year, they were among the best-performing investments. Stocks had become so predictable that people forgot the risks. They forgot that stock market returns were not guaranteed and that the market was not a place to sink money that they could ill afford to lose.

Few people had foreseen the catastrophic collapse of the mortgage markets that would bring down well-known investment banks such as Bear Stearns and Lehman Brothers and that would trigger a credit draught and, consequently, the loss of more than 8 million jobs, which raised the total number of unemployed to 15 million persons. Just before the downturn, the public mood was optimistic. The economy appeared to be booming. The unemployment rate was at 4.7%, and the rate had been below 5% for 23 consecutive months. Housing prices were rising along with stock prices. With the rate of home ownership greater than 65%, the appreciation made people feel rich. They took out home equity loans to buy cars and vacation villas. The future looked golden.

On October 9, 2007, the DJIA hit a high of 14,164.53. That same day, the S&P 500 had made an all-time high of 1565.15. Popular MSN MoneyCentral blogger Jon Markman captured the narcoleptic euphoria of the pre-recession era in May 2007 when he guaranteed his readers that the DJIA would climb significantly higher. He wrote, "Unless the world economic system completely runs off the rails, Dow 21,000 by 2012 is a lock. And anyone who says that ain't so lives in a Neverland, where kids never grow up, companies never innovate, consumers stop buying stuff, and home sweet home is a bomb shelter." That bit of juvenile sarcasm turned out to be closer to the truth than Markman or anyone else ever could have imagined. The market did run off its rails. In 2008, the DJIA fell 37.8%, its worst swoon since the

1930s. The S&P 500 tumbled 36.6%, which was its third worst year on record. The NASDAQ plunged by 40.5%. And this was only the first act of the investment horror show. A year after the market peak, on October 9, 2008, the DJIA closed at 8579.19. The DJIA kept falling in 2009, finally hitting a bottom on March 6, 2009 when it closed at 6547.05, a level it had last seen on April 15, 1997. Billions in savings had been wiped out. The unemployment rate was at 8.6%—the highest level in 26 years—and would reach 10% before the year was out.[5]

So it was with a vengeance that the investing public relearned that the market can be an unforgiving place. During the Great Recession, not even highly diversified mutual funds provided shelter from the economic storm. Diversification didn't work when stocks and bonds and real estate were dropping in tandem.

The downturn had been especially brutal for the large contingent of baby boomers who had been planning for a comfortable retirement funded by their pension and 401(K) accounts. The oft-repeated, grim humor of the day was that their 401(K) plans had become 201(K) plans.

Boomers frantically liquidated what was left of their stock holdings and shifted the proceeds into the safest, most predictable investments available, including Treasury securities with negative yields when adjusted for inflation. In the words of mordant pundits, these investors were looking for the return of their capital as opposed to a return on their capital.

The March 2009 market recovery came as a surprise. There was no fundamental reason for the bulls to be running. In fact, their buying portended the end of the recession three months later.

The actual nature of a recovery was a matter of intense debate among bulls, bears, and super bears even before many recognized that the recession had ended. The most optimistic economists, and there were not many of them, predicted a V-shaped economic rebound, meaning that economic activity would pick up as quickly as it had come down in 2007 and 2008 during the credit and housing crisis. In their view, the market rally reflected this outcome and thus was behaving rationally by bouncing back up like a super ball.

The conventional view was a pessimistic one. This broad camp argued that the recovery would be U-shaped, with slow gross domestic product (GDP) growth and high unemployment into the early years of the next decade. In their view, the stock markets were prematurely optimistic, the result of wishful thinking as opposed to solid earnings. There were some suspicions among this gloomy tribe that banks and Wall Street firms had been bidding up the price of stocks by trading them back and forth among themselves.[6] Such activity would generate higher returns for their substantial reserves of cash, which they were reluctant to lend, owing to economic conditions. It also would have boosted their capital positions.

A third, super-bearish contingent of economists predicted that the economy would sputter and then conk out sometime in 2010 as federal stimulus dollars diminished, a phenomenon they described as a double-dip recession. Some of them said the second leg of the slowdown might drag the country into a depression.

The endless debate among economists and market gurus, carried almost daily on the business pages, heightened the skittishness of investors. Yet many of them crept back into the market in April because of a greater fear they might miss a ride on a profitable post-recession bull market that would enable them to put their 2007 to 2008 losses behind them. They were desperate to recoup their savings. And they remembered tales by their great grandfathers about the Great Depression and the fortunes that were made by investors who had jumped into the market after it had crashed. Given their nervous condition, however, it would not take much of a fright to send them scrambling back to the sidelines.

Fast-forward to May 6, 2010, a day with nerve-jangling headlines. The citizens of nearly bankrupt Greece were rioting, casting doubts on the future of the Euro. There was an election in Great Britain that would have a material effect on its economic prospects. Millions of gallons of crude oil were spewing from a broken BP wellhead nearly a mile under the waters of the Gulf of Mexico, threatening unspeakable damage to one of the world's most magnificent marine habitats and disaster for the tourist and fishing industries of at least four states. The DJIA, which had been at 11,151.83 just three days earlier, had closed on April 5 at 10,868.12. Investors who had been creeping back into the market were worried and began to take some profits, which seemed the wise thing to do. Some commentators were predicting that events in Europe might tip the world's economy back into a deep recession.

Then at 2:30 p.m. EDT occurred one of the most bizarre and mysterious meltdowns in stock market history, an event destined to become known as the Flash Crash.[7] The DJIA plunged more than 700 points in ten minutes, its largest one-day fall ever. Then in the next ten minutes, it began to recover. The speed at which the event transpired was both stunning and alarming. There had been other one-day market plunges, most notably Black Monday in October 1987. But the regulators supposedly had fixed the markets after that staggering event so that nothing like it could ever happen again. This infamous day on May 6 showed investors that the equities market had become explosively volatile and that they could be wiped out in a matter of seconds. And it raised suspicions that the event had been deliberate, engineered by a new breed of market player, the so-called high-frequency traders. These tech-savvy traders pitted a new generation of computing machines against human investors, and the machines always seemed to win.

Some of the same physicists and mathematicians who had designed the exotic, synthetic mortgage securities that had wrecked havoc on the world's credit markets in 2007 and 2008 were now day-trading millions of shares of stocks, holding on to them for 2 minutes or less to make a fraction of a penny here and a fraction there, which at the end of the day added up to real money. Data showed that an estimated 73% of all U.S. equity trades involved high-frequency traders, who could execute an order in milliseconds.[8]

They thrived on volatility, which is anathema to long-term investors; and the suspicion was that the high-frequency traders were somehow at the bottom of the increasingly extreme, intraday market moves, using their superior technology and algorithms to manipulate stock prices. Even more disconcerting, the exchanges were selling these traders unfair advantages. In a real-life version of *The Sting*, these high-frequency traders knew of the prices of stocks and the direction of the market before the data was posted on the *ticker*—the consolidated tape that supplies the data to the public. It's small wonder then that retail investors took their money and ran for the doors immediately following the Flash Crash. Some headed back to bonds. Retail day traders, who bought and sold shares dozens of times each session, shifted their focus to the commodities markets, reasoning that if the stock market had become as risky as a pork bellies pit, they might as well go over to the CME, formerly known as the Commodities Mercantile Exchange (CME), where margins and taxes were more attractive, and play with its stock index futures. So many retail day traders made the switch that Ameritrade began introducing new commodities services aimed specifically at them. It was the firm's most robust area of growth.

"We see things commonly now that we didn't see 6 months ago," said Chris Nagy, managing director of routing order strategy for Ameritrade during a September 2010 interview. He went on, "Retail traders who sometimes acted as equity market specialists were saying, 'This market isn't fair.'"

And most retail investors stayed on the sidelines through the fall because the volatility seemed more pronounced in the aftermath of the Flash Crash. Economist Ed Yardeni perfectly captured retail investors' mood when he wrote in his August 5, 2010 newsletter, "The stock market has been exhibiting bipolar symptoms in recent months with intense mood swings from mania to depression and back. ...Since the S&P 500 peaked on April 23 through yesterday, it has been down 38 days and up 33 days. During the down days it lost a whopping 527 points. During the up days it gained 437 points. Over the same period, the DJIA lost 4,231 points during the 37 down days and gained a total of 3,708 points during the 34 up days. All that commotion, with so little motion one way or the other, has generated lots of swings between bearish and bullish emotion, leaving most investors exhausted."

In fact, the markets would never be the same. Well-intentioned regulators and lawmakers had meddled with market structure over the years and inadvertently changed what had been considered a national treasure into a casino dominated by unpredictable, high-speed computers. The Flash Crash was a symptom of the mess they had made.

This book tells the real story of the Flash Crash and its causes—one that you will not find in the official government accounts. It describes how Congress and the Securities and Exchange Commission, or SEC, beginning in the early 1970s played God with the market, setting out to create a paradise for long-term investors and inadvertently changed it into a financial purgatory. Blind in their belief that automation would make the markets fairer and more efficient, they inadvertently wrecked one of the world's great capital-allocation and job-creation engines and turned it into a wild playground for algorithmic traders. Initial public offerings of new, dynamic companies have all but disappeared. Capital, the lifeblood of the economy, is flowing into less productive assets, such as government bonds, precious metals, and third-world countries. And investors remain sidelined because the market is now the equivalent of a crapshoot.

Endnotes

1. Historical Index Data, *The Wall Street Journal* online (July 2, 2010).

2. Report of the staffs of the CFTC and SEC to the Joint Advisory Committee on Emerging Regulatory Issues, "Preliminary Findings Regarding the Market Events of May 6, 2010," Washington, DC (2010): 12–13.

3. Clemens Kownatzki, "Here's Why You Are Getting Sick from the Markets," Clemens Kownatzki's Instablog (2010), http://seekingalpha.com/author/clemens-kownatzki/instablog.

4. Tom Lauricella, "Dow Slides 10% in a Volatile Quarter," *The Wall Street Journal*, July 1, 2010.

5. According to the Bureau of Labor Statistics, the unemployment rate was 8.8% in October 1983.

6. Rodrigue Tremblay, "The Great Fed-Financed Dollar Decline and Stock Market Rally of 2009," http://www.globalresearch.ca/index.php?context=va&aid=15350.

7. All times are reported as Eastern Daylight Time.

8. Robert Iati, Adam Sussman, and Larry Tabb, "US Equity High-Frequency Trading: Strategies, Sizing, and Market Structure," VO7:023, September 2009 (www.tabbgroup.com): 14.

1

Strange Encounters

Beginning in 2007, two long-time equities traders named Sal Arnuk and Joseph Saluzzi noticed some weirdly disturbing price movements in the stock markets as they observed client trades on their multiple screens in a small trading room in quiet Chatham, New Jersey. When they went to hit a bid on certain exchanges, the price suddenly disappeared and a lower bid instantly appeared in its place. It was as though some invisible, malign force was attempting to trick the traders into chasing the stock up or down the price ladder. Never before had they seen anything like it. The ghostly presence was so incredibly fast that there was absolutely no chance of the traders ever winning the game. The deck was stacked against them. If they took the bait, they would always end up paying more or getting less than the market's consolidated tape of prices had initially advertized.

The price jumps were aggravating. Arnuk's and Saluzzi's job was to obtain the best execution price on large orders of shares for their institutional clients, which included large mutual fund managers such as INVESCO. Somebody was threatening their livelihood. Their firm, Themis Trading LLC, was named for a Greek goddess who personified fairness and trust.[1] Someone subtly was trying to subtract these two attributes from the market, and this got their blood boiling. It also got them wondering how the bastard was doing it.

The blocks of stock handled by Arnuk and Saluzzi were not small potatoes. They frequently ranged in size from 300,000 shares to 2 million shares. The transactions had to be conducted gingerly to avoid

"information leakage" that could cause imbalances in the market, raising the cost of transacting the business. The stock market always had
provided a habitat for predators who exploited weaknesses and inefficiencies in its structure, and if you did not avoid these cold-hearted
traders, you had about as much chance as an anchovy in a shark tank.
The game of hide and seek was relentless. The predators always were
probing for new weaknesses. If, for instance, the predators discovered
through the grapevine that a seller had a huge inventory of stock to
unload, they would short the stock, sending its price lower and costing
the institution precious nickels, dimes, and pennies. If they discovered
that a mutual fund or a pension fund was attempting to accumulate a
large position in a stock, they would front-run the order, buying up the
shares ahead of the bigger buyer and then selling it to them for a cent or
two more than it would have paid if its intentions had remained secret.

To avoid predation, cagey traders like Arnuk and Saluzzi
employed numerous strategies to camouflage both their identities
and their order size. If a big mutual fund wanted to sell several hundred thousand shares of a stock to rebalance its portfolio, it might use
a trusted broker as an intermediary to locate another, equally large
institution to buy its position at a negotiated price. It was hush-hush.
Blabbermouths were excluded from such arrangements.

If a large counterparty could not be found, the fund's traders
might take a portion of the order to a so-called *dark pool*, an off-
exchange venue where block traders anonymously submit buy and
sell orders, hoping to get at least a portion of the order executed.
Some dark pools were exclusive. Participants were expected to be fair
and honest, and any violation of the rules could result in immediate
suspension or even permanent expulsion. Because the bid and offers
in a dark pool were not posted in the public or "lit" markets, they did
not affect the prices on the consolidated quote. The public or lit market had no idea that a seller was looking for buyers and vice versa
until stock was actually sold. Then the execution price was listed on
the *consolidated tape*—the data feed one sees crawling across the
bottom of CNBC.

To sell the remaining shares, the fund often resorted to auto-mated trading software to break up the block into smaller orders, which then were sent to the various lit exchanges. The size and fre-quency of the orders was determined by algorithms looking at price and volume and the time parameters of the transaction. Finally, the funds and institutions enlisted the aid of human traders such as Arnuk and Saluzzi to use their wiles to avoid the predators.

Each of the methods had an Achilles' heel. For instance, there were limits on order sizes at the dark pools. And the algorithms that were employed to slice and dice big orders could be reverse-engi-neered in a matter of milliseconds by a predator's faster, more sophis-ticated algorithm, allowing it to automatically front-run the order. In the course of a year, a millisecond advantage for a high-frequency trader over the institutional traders can be worth $100 million.[2]

The funny business detected by Arnuk and Saluzzi was on a much higher level than the usual pitfalls that traders faced. The flickering prices were so radical that it was like a squadron of F-16 fighter jets suddenly appearing among the Sopwith Camels of World War I. Iron-ically, the phenomenon had appeared just about the time the U.S. Securities and Exchange Commission (SEC) had implemented its Regulation NMS (National Market System)—a sweeping reform aimed at increasing competition among the exchanges to both decrease customer costs and make the stock market friendlier to long-term investors. The rule, demanded by Congress in 1975, finally had been produced by the SEC 30 years later in 2005 and activated 2 years after that. Clearly, there was a link. Intrigued, the two traders decided to dig into the matter.

Arnuk and Saluzzi had not been spoiling for a fight or longing for the limelight. They had no idea what they were getting into and no premonition that their discovery would rattle the investment world. Since 2002, both had been living the good life in the upscale subur-ban community of Chatham, a rustic borough tucked off a highway near the uber-chic Short Hills Mall. Take the exit off of Route 24 by

Neiman Marcus and, behold, you were on Main Street in *Leave It to Beaver* land, with handsome, 1940s-era wood houses, tree-lined streets, and neatly trimmed lawns. Chatham was just 25 miles from Wall Street, but it might as well have been 10,000 miles away. None of Lower Manhattan's furious rush was evidenced here. There were no throngs of sharp-elbowed, driven people barreling down sidewalks, no blaring taxis clogging the streets. During the week, it seemed as quiet as Sunday.

Both men were veterans of Wall Street. After a decade working for big firms, they had traded a 2-hour round-trip commute between Manhattan and Brooklyn for a 10-minute, round-trip commute that saved them enough time to coach their kids' Little League games.[3] This was a utopia. They could balance their priorities of breadwinning and parenting with no maddening traffic jams and crowded subways in between.

They leased an office in a quaint, wooden retail village in the heart of town, opposite a dance studio, a tea restaurant, a tennis shop, and a beauty salon. It was not the locale usually associated with a trading floor. Their space was open and airy and had big windows on three walls to let the sun shine in. If they hadn't taken the space, it probably would have been occupied by a real estate office or a small accounting firm.

Inside, it had the air of a man cave, with golf clubs leaning against the wall. Arnuk and Saluzzi and three other traders dressed their Saturday's best: dungarees or shorts, and tee shirts. And there were lots of computers. Their "trading floor" was a long desk topped with four or five multiscreened computer screens where they watched the world, the markets, and their clients buy and sell orders and talked about the frustrating New York Mets between trades.

Both men love baseball, although neither played beyond the youth-league level. As adults, they both coached their sons' teams with passion. Arnuk, who had attended the prestigious Poly Prep high school in Brooklyn, a private high school whose alumni include former SEC Chairman Arthur Levitt, had bonded with his father and siblings as he grew up watching baseball on a black-and-white television. He also bonded with his own kids through baseball. Arnuk was a sturdy, soft-spoken man who wore black-rimmed glasses and looked like a professor. His calm exterior belied his highly competitive side. Saluzzi, who had attended Bishop Ford High School in Brooklyn, carried himself like a ball player. He was trim and walked with a relaxed, sure-footed gait.

The Brooklyn natives went a long way back and appeared to be as close as brothers. They had met in the late 1980s at Morgan Stanley, their first employer after college. Arnuk, who grew up in Brooklyn's Bay Ridge section, had a BA in finance from SUNY Binghamton University; and Saluzzi, who hailed from the Sheepshead Bay neighborhood, had a BA in finance from NYU. After a few years at the prestigious firm, they both concluded independently that to advance in the world of finance, they'd have to obtain graduate degrees. So they both left Morgan Stanley to enroll in MBA programs. Arnuk started attending the Stern School of Business at NYU part time; and Saluzzi resigned a few months later to attend the Kenan-Flagler Business School of the University of North Carolina.

Arnuk graduated in 1991, and Saluzzi in 1993. Arnuk began working for Instinet, a global brokerage firm that specialized in computerized trading. He recruited Saluzzi for a job there. They were neighbors at this point. Both men had married and secured homes in Bay Ridge.

In 2002, Saluzzi and Arnuk got tired of the rat race and decided to move to New Jersey and start their own company. Arnuk was the first to go, and he convinced Saluzzi to join him in a trading venture.

They were not making the kind of big money that drives a congressman to denounce Wall Street from the floor of the House or the Senate, but they were not doing badly either. The business wasn't exclusively about money anyway. They were self-sufficient. They were their own bosses. But in 2007, someone was threatening their business by playing unfairly. It was like a ball player shooting up on steroids so he could muscle the ball farther than anyone else.

Someone in the market was using the equivalent of steroids to trade in and out of the market faster than everybody else.

As the men began to track down the hombre, they learned just how radically Regulation NMS had changed the market, and it surprised them. The change had engendered an explosion in the number of high-frequency traders plying the markets with super-charged computers and advanced pattern-recognition and statistical software designed to beat the market. These guys always had been around, but now there seemed to be a lot more of them, and their robotic trading machines were much faster than anything ever deployed in the markets. They programmed these overclocked computers to make money buying and selling stocks without direct human oversight. For every dozen firms, there were hundreds of these robotic trading wunderkinds, and their numbers were growing every day because venture capitalists and hedge funds were bankrolling start-ups left and right. Clearly, a lot of people thought high-frequency trading (HFT) was a path to quick and easy profits.

The general investment public had no idea that this market version of the *Invasion of the Body Snatchers* was under way. Some of the biggest players in the high-frequency trading sector were not household names: They were proprietary trading firms such as Getco and Tradebot and hedge funds such as Millennium, DE Shaw, WorldQuant, and Renaissance Technologies. Others were household names, but investors hadn't paid much attention to their forays into mechanized trading because it was a relatively small portion of their earnings and they did not break out the numbers in their annual reports. Goldman Sachs, which had become notorious in the public's eyes, owing to its role in the collapse of the mortgage market, had a sizable high-frequency trading desk. Registered brokers like Bank of America and Lime Brokerage and Credit Suisse offered suites of exotic trading algorithms and other services to customers who wanted to engage in the practice. But they all were secretive about the success of these operations. Why tempt copycats?

Joining the gold rush were commodities traders and teams of computer scientists and mathematicians with formulas designed to outsmart any human trader. The human brain was not smart enough or quick enough to compete with the over-clocked, nitrogen-cooled computing engines designed by whiz kids and trading hundreds of millions of stock shares every day. The trader-scientists began writing algorithms so that their computers could outsmart competing trading computers, triggering the equivalent of an arms race. Teams of mathematicians and computer scientists worked round-the-clock to improve their machines.

Arnuk and Saluzzi discovered that these new competitors had another significant technological advantage: Most of them possessed servers that were "collocated" at or near the exchanges. This meant that for a steep, monthly rental, a high-frequency trading firm was allowed to link its servers directly to the servers of the stock exchanges and get price and trading data milliseconds faster than anyone who could not or would not spring for such a hookup, like retail investors. In the view of the HFT crowd, this "low-latency" networking was completely within the bounds of acceptable behavior. Alistair Brown, founder of Lime Brokerage, which caters to high-frequency traders, said in a magazine interview in 2007, "Any *fair* market is going to select the best price from the buyer or seller who gets their order in their first. Speed definitely becomes an issue. If everyone has access to the same information, when the market moves, you want to be the first. The people who are too slow are going to be left behind."[4]

Depending on which strategies they employed, the HFT firms programmed their computers to hold the stocks anywhere from 2 minutes to 2 days. Their object was to make a little money on each trade, not swing for the fence. It was a fairly predictable business because the shorter the period of time under study, the easier it is to forecast the future based on historic pricing, volume, and other data. Systems become increasingly unstable over time, which is why long-range weather forecasts are unreliable and which is why hedge funds making multiyear credit bets lost their shirts in 2007. The lesson of 2007 had made a deep impression on so-called quants, which was short for "quantitative investors." They embraced HFT with religious fervor. Less risk equaled more money. The founder of Tradebot, an HFT located in Kansas City, Missouri, told students in 2008 that his firm typically held stocks for 11 seconds and had not suffered a losing day in four years.[5]

There was no public source of information of HFT industry profits, just anecdotes and rumors, so no one knew for certain how much money they were pulling down in a given year. The best conservative estimate was $20 billion just for firms that tried to earn small spreads and fees from the exchanges by playing the role of market maker. They represented less than 10% of the HFT universe.

A market maker takes the opposite side of an incoming order to earn a small profit on the spread on fees. Often this is less than 2 cents per share. But if the HFT firm trades millions of shares each day, it can rack up a handsome annual return. Some earn returns of close to 300%.

By December 2008, Saluzzi and Arnuk had a strong suspicion as to what was going on in the markets. Like all good investigators, they had cultivated inside sources from a number of HFT firms. What they found was disturbing: Based on their reading of the facts, high-frequency shops were using their superior computing power in new, devious, and possibly unethical ways to covertly attack institutional customers and consequently raise their trading costs. Some of the strategies looked like bare-faced attempts to manipulate the market. Arnuk and Saluzzi detected signs of *momentum ignition*, in which an algorithm initiates a series of trades in an attempt to trick other machines into believing that a particular stock is headed higher or lower; and *spoofing*, a practice in which the machines feign interest in buying or selling a stock to manipulate its price. The victims of these questionable techniques included mutual funds and pensions, so in the final analysis, it was the small investor who was getting nicked by this new iteration of Wall Street avarice. No one had noticed—least of all the SEC and examiners at the Financial Industry Regulatory Authority (FINRA), an industry-financed outfit charged with policing brokers and the stock exchanges. The SEC staff members had so little day-to-day personal contact with Wall Street professionals that they knew almost nothing about what was really happening there beyond the direction of the stock averages. They relied on FINRA, which had a reputation of being less than diligent.

Arnuk and Saluzzi were not politically connected. Theirs was a small-fry firm. But they felt compelled to sound an alarm and bring their suspicions to the attention of the broader investing public. Something was askew in the marketplace. So the men elected to disseminate their findings in a white paper to their 30 institutional clients and then post the paper on their blog. Those clients typically ran just 2% to 5% of their order flow through Themis Trading. Arnuk and Saluzzi figured the clients were losing lots of money to high-frequency traders on the remainder of the order flow transacted elsewhere because they were unaware of what was going on.

They titled their paper "Toxic Equity Trading Order Flow on Wall Street: The Real Force Behind the Explosion in Volume and Volatility." The white paper read more like an op-ed piece than the academic treatise suggested by its title. Arnuk and Saluzzi offered no empirical evidence, just their hunches. Hard evidence was tough to come by; no one, not even HFT consultant Tabb Group, could say with absolute certainty how many HFT firms existed. The HFT corner of the market was unregulated. It was also guarded. Traders worked behind closed doors with upmost secrecy to protect their "secret sauces," the algorithms that they used to outsmart other traders. The duo did have 40 years of combined trading experience, however. They understood the mechanics of the market, and they had seen hundreds of schemes designed to take advantage of unwary investors. And they had their snitches. They were convinced that such scheming was occurring now on a grand scale.

The white paper asserted that the explosion in market volatility that most people ascribed to the global financial crisis that had begun in August 2007 was largely the product of high-frequency traders who had invaded the market *en masse* to exploit changes wrought by SEC's new rules.

"The number of quote changes has exploded," they wrote. "The reason is high-frequency traders searching for hidden liquidity. Some estimates are that these traders enter anywhere from several hundred to one million orders for every 100 trades they actually execute." HFT machines would enter an order and cancel it almost immediately, just to see if there was buying interest at a particular price level. Arnuk and Saluzzi referred to this practice as *pinging*, conjuring the image of a destroyer conducting a sonar sweep for a hidden submarine. High-frequency trading computers would issue an order ultra-fast away from the listed price of a stock, and if nothing happened, they would cancel it immediately and send out another. The machines were looking for hidden information to use to their advantage, such as whether there were big institutional customers afoot trying to fill large orders.

The strategy was cunning. Say there was an institutional trader who had instructed a computer to purchase shares of a stock for between $20.00 and $20.03, but no higher. Theoretically, no one else in the marketplace would know this. The high-frequency trader's algorithm, however, might recognize that a pattern of purchases for the particular stock's shares at $20 was typical of algorithms employed by institutions accumulating a large position. So the HFT algorithm would ping the institution's algorithm, offering perhaps to sell 100 shares of the stock to the institution at $20.05. If nothing were to happen, the HFT algorithm immediately would cancel the trade and offer 100 shares at $20.04. If nothing again happened, it would cancel and offer $20.03. If the institution's algorithm were to buy the stock, the HFT algorithm would know that it had found a buyer willing to pay up to $20.03 for a stock listed at $20. The HFT algorithm then quickly plunged back into the market offering to buy the same stock at a penny above the institution's original $20.00 bid. Then it would turn around and continuously sell those shares to the institution's algorithm at $20.03. That extra penny, Arnuk and Saluzzi asserted, amounted to a "stealth tax" on retail and institutional investors.

Most investors—retail lambs and the large, bovine institutional traders—didn't realize that they were being bled because it was a death by a thousand cuts as opposed to a pneumatically propelled bolt to the forehead. They had no way of knowing that an uninvited middleman had come between them and the stock market.

This sort of shenanigan had begun in 2007 because Regulation NMS took away the duopoly status of NASDAQ and the New York Stock Exchange (NYSE) by allowing any exchange to trade listed securities. Previously, the majority of trades on NYSE-listed stocks were done on the NYSE and NASDAQ-listed stocks in the NASDAQ market. New computerized exchanges proliferated, anxious to get a slice of NASDAQ's and the NYSE's lucrative business. To survive in the face of the new competition, NASDAQ and the NYSE were compelled to go public. Suddenly, they were accountable to stockholders who vocally demanded a decent return on their investment; so the once-dominant exchanges had to fight tooth and claw against the new competitors for the trade volume they had lost. They soon discovered deep-pocketed customers in the form of the high-frequency traders, who were arbitraging price inefficiencies among the dozen or so equity exchanges and between the equities markets and the commodities markets. The NYSE and the NASDAQ solicited the HFT business, as did all the other exchanges. They offered these prime customers special trading advantages as an inducement.

"Before 2007 and Regulation NMS, you really didn't have this high-frequency stuff," said Saluzzi. "The NYSE was still a slow market, and 80% of the trades were on the floor of the exchange. But once those trades migrated to newer, electronic exchanges, trading became fast. Overall market volume went from 3 billion shares to

10 billion shares because regulation NMS opened a whole new playground for high-frequency traders, and they went crazy."

Some of the exchanges offered the HFT firms rebates of subpennies-per-share for serving as market makers and buying stocks from other customers. Buy and sell tens of millions of shares a day, and that fraction of a cent adds up to substantial profit. Arnuk and Saluzzi said in their white paper that the rebate scheme inadvertently led to what they termed *hot-potato trading* that inflated market volume statistics and made the market seem much more liquid than it was.

"If two guys trade 1,000 shares back and forth a million times, that's a billion shares. Did a billion shares actually trade, or did the thousand shares change hands a million times between two guys playing hot potato? We argue that the real volume is 1,000 shares."

The volume, real or not, generated data for the consolidated tape, which in turn was a marketable product. The more data that an exchange generated for the tape at year end, the bigger its share of the revenues from sales of that data to information vendors and brokerages. So they were not about to crack down on this practice.

Saluzzi and Arnuk charged that the high-frequency traders were playing other games as well, all because they were able to move faster than everyone else. In part, it was because the NYSE and the NASDAQ had invited them to collocate their servers close to the exchange's servers. This arrangement reduced the time required to get an order executed. The cost ranged from $1,500 to $50,000 per month for each server cabinet. There also was an installation charge that ran anywhere from $5,000 to $50,000. The NYSE was so grateful for the new business that it took steps in October 2007 to make it easier for program traders to move the markets higher and lower. The NYSE publicly removed curbs that shut down the program trading if the market moved more than two percent in any direction, the white paper stated. NYSE asserted that the approach to limiting market volatility envisioned by the use of the "trading collars" was not as meaningful today as it had been in the late 1980s when the rules were adopted. The rules had been put in place in 1987 following Black Monday, the largest one-day crash since the Great Depression. The white paper said, "On a more commercial level, the NYSE had been at a competitive disadvantage because other market centers that didn't have curbs were getting the program trading business."

One nefarious-sounding strategy, cited by the white paper, was designed to quickly move the price of a share higher by 10 to 15 cents by employing a handful of 100- to- 500- share trades executed in rapid succession. Then the high-frequency trader would suddenly short the stock, knowing full well he had artificially pumped up the price and that it shortly would begin to fall.

In a fictional example by the authors, an institutional buyer is trying to accumulate stock between $20 and $20.10 per share. Using the same techniques as the rebate trader, a high-frequency trader spots the $20 bid as an institutional order. When the institution next bids $20.01, the high-frequency trader buys stock at $20.02, driving up the price. The institution follows and buys more shares at $20.02. The high-frequency trader in this matter runs the stock up to $20.10 per share, with the institution chasing the stock. At this point, the high-frequency traders also stock short at $20.10 knowing it is highly likely that the price of the stock will fall back to the low $20 range.

Finally, the two traders accused their high-frequency competition of a sin known in the parlance of the industry as *momentum ignition*. The high-frequency traders engage this strategy to juice a market already moving up or down, creating either a major decline or a big upward spike in prices. A trader could rapidly submit and cancel many orders, and execute some actual trades to "spoof" the algorithms of other traders into action and cause them to buy or sell more aggressively. Or the trader might try to trigger some standing stop loss orders that would cause a price decline. By establishing a position early on, the trader could profit by liquidating the position if he is successful in igniting a price movement. This strategy might be most effective in less actively traded stocks, which receive little help and public attention and are vulnerable to price movements sparked by a relatively small amount of volume.[6]

After sending the paper to clients, Arnuk and Saluzzi posted a copy of the white paper on their blog site, where they expected its contents to be discovered by the larger investing world and then widely disseminated and discussed. That, after all, was the way things regularly happened on the World Wide Web, wasn't it?

"We were not trying to make a name for ourselves," Arnuk said later. "All that we wanted to do was fix what was wrong. We were sharing it with our customers so they could improve what they were doing when they traded away from us."

The charges by Arnuk and Saluzzi were sensational and potentially explosive. The markets were being manipulated. No one else had noticed what they had noticed. Regulators had been asleep. They hadn't blown any time-out whistles or thrown any penalty flags for spoofing or momentum ignition or pinging. This was outrageous, because the SEC and FINRA were supposed to be cleaning up their act after missing abuses like Bernie Madoff's outrageous Ponzi scheme.

But after the two traders disseminated the white paper, nothing happened—nothing at all. Investors in December 2008 had other things on their minds. They were consumed by bailouts, failures, bankruptcies, and the incoming Democratic administration of Barack Obama. The white paper was little more than background noise.

"Outside of our clients, no one made a stink or even mentioned our findings," recalled Arnuk.[7]

The two men may have been disappointed, but they were not quitters. For them, this was personal. The HFT firms were a threat to their way of life. They continued to plug away, albeit in relative obscurity. In a prescient, follow-up white paper published in early July, Arnuk and Saluzzi warned of the possibility of a lightning-fast market collapse induced by high-frequency traders with unfiltered connections to the stock exchanges through so-called "sponsored access agreements" with a registered broker. The brokers essentially vouched for the integrity of their customers without doing real due diligence. The firms might be thinly capitalized or controlled by criminals, for all the regulators knew.

"Many of these arrangements do not have any pre-trade risk controls since these clients demand the fastest speed. Due to the fully electronic nature of the equity markets today, one keypunch error could wreak havoc. Nothing would be able to stop a market destroying order once the button was pressed," they wrote.

Once again, few people paid attention. It sounded shrill and far-fetched, like the Y2K scare that had predicted a meltdown of computers worldwide on January 1, 2000 because twentieth-century computer programs would not recognize dates after 1999. This apathy about their white paper would begin to evaporate days later as a result of a quasi-comic confluence of events involving the FBI, short-tempered Wall Street bankers, a Bulgarian-born blogger, and a preening U.S. senator.

Endnotes

1. Kate Welling, "Playing Fair?," welling@weeden, June 11, 2010.

2. Richard Martin, "Wall Street's Quest to Process Data at the Speed of Light," *InformationWeek*, April 21, 2007.

3. Kate Welling, "Playing Fair?," welling@weeden, June 11, 2010.

4. Richard Martin, "Data Latency Having an Ever Increasing Role in Effective Trading," *InformationWeek*, May 25, 2007.

5. Stephen Gandel, "Is KC Firm the New King of Wall Street?," Curious Capital blogs, *Time Magazine*, May 18, 2010.

6. Securities and Exchange Commission, "Concept Release on Equity Market Structure: Proposed Rule," *The Federal Register* (January 21, 2010) 3609.

7. Author interview in June 2010.

2

Not Your Grandma's Market

The change in the investment landscape wrought by Regulation National Market System (NMS) had occurred so quickly that it escaped the notice of the average investor. He had not been asleep like some Rip Van Winkle; but neither had he been paying close attention to what was going on. As far as he was concerned, the market was the same as it had always been. In his mind, there were two major exchanges, the New York Stock Exchange (NYSE) or "Big Board," and the NASDAQ. In actuality, there were about a dozen exchanges and several hundred other trading venues. The retail investor submitted his order to a broker and received a trade confirmation within minutes. The investor didn't consider that the NYSE-listed stock he was buying had been sold to him through his own broker or in a dark pool or on some stock exchange that he had never heard of like BATS or Direct Edge or the National Stock Exchange. He had no idea how the broker had routed his order, and he didn't much care. Had the investor bothered to look, he would have been shocked to see how radically the markets had been altered by electronics and increased competition. Had he tried to track one of his trades, he would have been mystified.

The U.S. Commodities markets had come into the modern age more quickly than the equities markets. The Commodities Futures Trading Commission (CFTC), which regulated that end of the investment universe, didn't try to micromanage its markets the way the Securities and Exchange Commission (SEC) did. Since 2000, the

CFTC had been relying solely on "principle's based" regulation. In the words of former CFTC chairman Walt Lukken, "A principles-based system requires markets to meet certain public outcomes in conducting their business operations. For example, U.S. futures exchanges must continuously meet 18 core principles—ranging from maintaining adequate financial safeguards to conducting market surveillance—in order to uphold their good standing as a regulated contract market. Such an approach has the advantage of being flexible for both regulator and regulated. As technology and market conditions change, exchanges may discover more effective ways to meet a mandated principle."

The commodities exchanges were forced to transition from human-intermediated venues, where traders vied with one another in trading pits, to computers early in the new century because of competition from European exchanges. Commodities regulators had lowered barriers to foreign competitors as quid pro quo for European governments allowing American commodities exchanges to compete in the Old World.

Before the appearance of the Europeans on U.S. soil, there had been four major commodities exchanges and several smaller, specialized, regional exchanges. All of them had been owned mutually by their trading members. The largest exchanges were the Chicago Mercantile Exchange (CME); the Chicago Board of Trade (CBOT); the New York Mercantile Exchange; and the New York Board of Trade. Throughout the 1990s when computerized trading began to spread owing to the introduction of more sophisticated personal computers, these exchanges resisted the transformation to electronic trading simply because that threatened the livelihood of their owners.

The CBOT was the oldest exchange, established in 1847. At its founding, it specialized in wheat and oat futures. In the twentieth century, it proved to be one of the most innovative exchanges in the world, introducing U.S. Treasury futures in 1975 and later, financial options and futures on the Dow Jones Industrial Average (DJIA), which became invaluable hedging tools for finance professionals.

The CME spun itself off from the CBOT in 1898 as the Chicago Butter and Egg Board. The founders redubbed it the CME in 1919 because it was trading other agricultural commodities by then. The twentieth century was an era of innovation for the CME as well. The exchange introduced pork belly futures in 1961, live cattle futures in 1964, the first futures on foreign currencies in 1972 (which was the year after Nixon suspended the dollar's convertibility into gold and destroyed the Bretton Woods system), and stock index futures in 1982.

The New York Mercantile Exchange, or "The Merc," and its subsidiary the "Comex" began in the 1870s as a butter and egg exchange and branched out into other agricultural products. By the late 1990s, the exchange also was trading precious metals, copper, oil, gas, uranium, and a host of other commodities.

The New York Board of Trade was best known to the public as the site of some of the scenes in the 1983 comedy hit *Trading Places*, which starred comedians Dan Aykroyd and Eddie Murphy. It was founded in 1870 as a cotton exchange and by the late 1990s was trading coffee, cocoa, cotton, ethanol, frozen concentrated orange juice, sugar, pulp, and foreign currencies.

The commodities exchanges had lasted 100 years almost unaltered because their regulatory structure made it expensive for competitors to enter the business. Each exchange had its own "clearing house," where trades were settled, and these were expensive operations.

When the deep-pocketed, fully automated European exchanges attempted to establish beachheads in New York and Chicago in the 1990s, America's exchanges suddenly appreciated their need to both modernize and consolidate.

Europe had seen the handwriting on the wall calling for change years earlier. The Germans and the Swiss were the first to establish electronic exchanges of any significant size. They merged their respective exchanges in 1998 to create Eurex, which specialized in financial futures, options, and other derivative products. The new exchange was so fast and efficient, and it began to squeeze the life out of the London International Financial Futures and Options Exchange, also known as LIFFE. LIFFE eventually adopted electronic trading, building a system that was even more advanced than the one wielded by Eurex. LIFFE survived, only to be swallowed up later by the NYSE. But this is getting ahead of the story.

When the LIFFE and Eurex set up shops in the United States, the CME adapted by becoming automated and demutualizing—buying out the traders who owned it and then issuing stock to the public to replace that capital. This infusion of money gave the CME the financial wherewithal to buy the CBOT, which simply did not adapt to the new electronic challengers in time to protect its market share. The CME also purchased the New York Merc. It eventually ended up controlling about 96% of the market. Eurex and LIFFE never gained enough traction in the U.S. market to make their continued presence here worthwhile.

The New York Board of Trade was bought out by Atlanta's Intercontinental Exchange (ICE) in 2006 for about $1 billion. ICE previously traded petroleum and energy futures and options contracts. The company took off after Enron, another energy trading company, collapsed due to a massive accounting fraud. In 2010, ICE was trying to become a big player in the credit derivative swaps market, which was being forced by the Congress in the aftermath of the 2007 credit collapse to move from unlit over-the-counter (OTC) trading markets to an exchange.

So on the commodities side of the market, competition caused consolidation. Most of the trading activity moved to the CME. It became the 800-pound gorilla, making the job of regulating those markets much easier. The commodities markets had traveled in the opposite direction of the equities market, where competition resulted in an explosion of trading venues.

Familiar names like the New York Stock Exchange and NASDAQ still existed on the equities side; and as far as your average investor knew, they remained the industry's dominant trading centers. This misperception was understandable. As recently as 2006, the duopoly had controlled 74.1% of equity market trading volume. And when an investor turned on a business news channel like Fox Business or CNBC, the backdrop of any trading report generally was the floor of the NYSE at 11 Wall Street, because it was the only equities exchange left that employed human intermediaries. But between 2007 and 2009, as Regulation NMS eased the entry and expansion of competing trading venues, the combined volume of the NYSE and NASDAQ shriveled to 50.8%.[1] In May 2010, the NYSE, which at its peak boasted of an 80% share of all the volume in NYSE listed stocks, reported a 21% market share.

Regulation NMS permitted brokerage houses to internalize trades as long as they matched the best price displayed on the consolidated tape. In fact, this is how 15% of all trades—including virtually 100% of all retail trades—are consummated. In 2010, there were more than 200 broker dealers engaged in the practice. Profits worldwide from the practice are estimated at $100 billion.[2] By way of comparison, 19.4% of all trades are on the NASDAQ Market, and 14.7% are on the NYSE.

The brokerage firm is happy to keep the trade in house because internalizing the order reduces its costs. Also, by keeping trades in house, the broker provides its own traders with an advanced look at the customer trade data before it is posted on the tape. The firm's traders can use this informational advantage to their benefit.

Stock exchanges and high-frequency traders complained bitterly that the brokerages had a virtual monopoly on retail trades, the most profitable trades of all. One high-frequency trader said, "Everybody wants to trade against retail order flow because it's uninformed. It's pretty juicy to trade against. You can pretty much take the other side of every order and make money every day." Most of the orders handled by the exchanges are "informed orders" from professional traders. In the parlance of the industry, these orders are dubbed "toxic" because they are usually limit-orders placed close to the bid price, which reduces the amount of spread enjoyed by a buyer or a seller.

High-frequency traders are queued up at an exchange waiting for orders. It's supposed to be first-come, first serve. But the brokerages, because of internalization, are able to step to the front merely by offering customers a one-hundredth-of-a-penny price improvement over the nationally displayed best bid or offer price for a specific stock. For example, if a stock is displayed on the consolidated tape at $10.00 bid and $10.02 asked, and a retail customer submits a market order, the broker can grab that order before it goes to an exchange merely by selling the customer the stock at $10.0199. What especially miffs the exchanges is that the brokers use their displayed prices as the basis to execute the trade internally.

On the rare occasion that a broker can't find an in-house counterparty for a customer order, the transaction is handed off to a middleman called an *executing broker*. This could be a firm such as UBS, Knight Capital, or ATD, or even a hedge fund such as Citadel. The executing broker decides whether it wants to take the other side of the brokerage customer's trade. If it doesn't, say because the spread is too narrow, the order is routed to a *dark pool*, an off-exchange venue where big institutional traders lurk anonymously, trying to buy or sell large amounts of stock without rippling the public or "lit" market. Many of the executing brokers own their own dark pools. If they can execute your trade there, they pay you a tenth-of-a-penny price improvement over the best offer price listed on the consolidated tape. If for some reason the executing broker cannot find a match in a dark pool, it sends your order, which in the parlance of the industry is called *exhaust*, to an exchange such as NASDAQ or the NYSE. All this happens in seconds.

Investors who want their shares to go directly to an exchange can request this, but some brokers charge an extra fee for the service.

The dramatic loss of business to these new competitors forced both the NYSE and NASDAQ to fight for customers, which was a brand new experience for them. Initially, both of the exchanges went on a shopping spree to purchase enough volume to stay afloat. The NYSE bought the American Stock Exchange and, seeing that the future would be given over to the machines, it also purchased an all-electronic venue called Archipelago, which had previously gobbled up the Pacific Stock Exchange. NASDAQ swallowed both the Philadelphia Stock Exchange, which had a lucrative options market, and the Boston Stock Exchange. Each purchased a European exchange to extend its reach overseas. In 2007, the NYSE Group, Inc. merged with Europe's Euronext N.V. to create NYSE Euronext. In February 2008, NASDAQ merged with Sweden's OMX exchange to create NASDAQ OMX.

NASDAQ had long ago migrated to electronics to conduct trading, replacing human market makers who had acted as middlemen in stock transactions between buyers and sellers, taking a markup as recompense. Some of them had proven to be less than honest, speeding the transition there from man to machine. The NYSE established a preserve of sorts for endangered flesh and blood market makers by electing to remake itself as a hybrid exchange. Half the operation was set up as a trading floor with 1,500 men and women working for five designated market makers: Barclays Capital; Bank America; Getco; Kellogg Specialist Group; and Spear, Leeds & Kellogg Specialists. The other half, NYSE ARCA, was all electronic. The NYSE's odd configuration was, in part, nostalgia for the good old days when as many as 4,500 persons working for 55 specialist firms intermediated

every trade for NYSE-listed securities and, in part, a marketing gim-
mick that counted on customers wanting a human intelligence in the
market to trade against the trend whenever chaos ensued.

The NYSE and NASDAQ, which had been owned by members,
followed the lead of the CME and became public companies—and
as such they no longer functioned like a cross between an old boys
club and a municipal utility. They now had to earn a decent return
for shareholders in a jungle-like business environment where competitors went at it, bloody tooth to bloody claw. There was a new
breed of traders known as high-frequency traders who were making
huge amounts of money, and the exchanges fought for their business
by offering concierge services, such as "collocation" of their computers at the exchange, right next to the exchange's own machines. This
allowed high-frequency traders to enter trades faster than most
everyone else. They were hooked on speed. They were physicists and
computer jocks who had designed algorithms to recognize trading
patterns that lasted just a few milliseconds, as short as the flicker of a
flame, and execute transactions to take advantage of them. There
were so many of them doing pretty much the same thing that an early
jump from the blocks had tremendous appeal, and they were quite
willing to pay up to $50,000 per month for that slight advantage.

Each exchange also began selling its unique pricing data directly to
the deep-pocketed high-frequency trading (HFT) customers so that
they could see it milliseconds before it was posted on the consolidated
tape, giving them an informational advantage over the general public
as well.

The irony of this was that in August 2000, the SEC had adopted
regulation FD, which stood for fair disclosure, to prevent, in the
agency's own words, "selective disclosure of information by publicly
traded companies and other issuers." When an issuer of stock disclosed material nonpublic information to a market professional such
as a stock analyst or a pension fund manager, it had to issue a release
sharing the information with the general public. The rule was

prompted by complaints about brokerage house lunches featuring analysts and corporate executives who shared news about the companies with select clients.

On the day the regulation was adopted, SEC Chairman Arthur Levitt said, "There's a saying that only three things matter in real estate: location, location, location. Unfortunately, in some quarters, the same principle is taking root in investing, and the place to be is inside the information loop—that small circle of Wall Street professionals with whom companies share significant nonpublic information before the rest of us. Like that neighborhood with gated entrances and tall fences, moving into the information loop is not always an option for many of America's small investors.

"Simply put, these practices defy the principles of integrity and fairness. In this country, we pride ourselves on having the purest form of meritocracy in the world. We teach our children that a person gets ahead through hard work and diligence. We ground ourselves in a trust that, through equal opportunity, everyone has a chance to succeed. America's marketplace should be no exception. Instead, it should serve as a beacon. No one should be excluded."

Granted, the exchanges were not issuers. But the practice of giving one class of investors a jump on everybody else seemed to mock the spirit of fair play espoused by Levitt. Ironically, in August 2009—almost 9 years to the day he espoused market democracy—Levitt wrote an op-ed for the *Wall Street Journal* defending the high-frequency traders, failing to note he was a paid consultant to several HFT firms. Levitt wrote, "The Securities and Exchange Commission should ignore these complaints and the caricature that has developed of high-frequency traders. These traders have developed systems to allow them to beat the competition to displayed quotes. They have taken available space near the markets' data servers to squeeze time out of every transaction. These traders continuously look for inefficiencies, and by exploiting them, correct them. I see nothing sinister or unfair about the advantages that come out of their investments and efforts."

A few exchanges went even further for HFT subscribers to their data feed and froze some customer orders for a few milliseconds to give them a first shot at taking them and earning a rebate for making the transaction. These were called *flash orders*. Dan Mathisson, managing director of advanced electronic systems at Credit Suisse, and a pioneer in algorithmic trading, said in his view, flash orders violated the spirit of regulation NMS and weakened the notion of a national market system.[3] Levitt also was in favor of banning that practice.

In effect, with the assistance of the exchanges, the high-frequency traders were driving around the markets in the equivalent of 1200-horsepower Bugatti Veyron Super Sport roadsters while retail investors whose brokers did not employ similarly sophisticated and expensive systems on their behalf were puttering around in the equivalent of the family sedan.

The market was so tilted in their favor that in March 2011, Credit Suisse saw a big business opportunity in launching a new kind of trading platform—an Electronic Communication Network (ECN) that had rules favoring institutional investors and disadvantaging high-frequency traders.

The SEC was so out of touch with the markets, it actually believed that the consolidated tape was the best source of information for the best prices in a listed security, precluding the need for investors to subscribe to data feeds from each of the 10 exchanges and 70-plus automated trading systems (ATS).[4] In fact, right under the SEC's nose, a duel market had developed: a high-end market for the moneyed traders and a low-end, less efficient market for retail investors. The SEC never noticed until Saluzzi and Arnuk got its attention in 2009.

Regulators also failed to grasp a more fundamental fact. Because the high-frequency traders were executing related trades simultaneously on all the stock venues and all the commodity venues, the equities and the commodities markets in effect had been unified. A trader sensing that inflation risks were growing, for example, simultaneously could buy gold and oil futures and short stocks and the dollar on multiple exchanges. Action in one corner would affect all other parts of the trading universe. It was as seamless as the World Wide Web, but the turf-obsessed regulators still viewed the world in terms of a single, distinct market for equities and a single, distinct market for commodities.

Delaware Democratic Theodore Kaufman, an SEC critic, bitterly complained, "Our regulators work in silos."[5]

"Responsibilities are divided between the SEC and the CFTC," he said in a floor speech. "Within equities markets we (also) have multiple self-regulatory organizations setting rules—more silos: New York Stock Exchange, NASDAQ, FINRA, the National Stock Exchange, and more...We created a *National Market System*, but we forgot to create a *National Regulatory and Surveillance System* to go along with it."

Because of this double vision, high-frequency traders had managed to hijack the market right under the nose of both agencies. They had thrived like kudzu under Regulation NMS even though the rule had been intended to make the market a venue for the allocation of long-term capital. Regulation NMS stated, "When the interests of long-term investors and short-term traders conflict..., the Commission believes that its clear responsibility is to uphold the interests of long-term investors."[6] Although high-frequency traders had brought some benefits to other investors, such as increased liquidity for stocks in the Standard & Poor's (S&P) 1000 and narrower spreads, it had come at a cost. Mutual funds and pensions had to pay for anti-gaming systems to keep the high-frequency boys from eating their lunch, costs that were passed on to retail investors. Furthermore, Flash Crash, which clearly was exacerbated by theses new players, had scared retail money out of the U.S. market. The little guy felt the U.S. equity market was rigged. He increasingly was investing overseas and in the commodities markets.

What was darkly humorous about these developments was that Regulation NMS had been 30 years in the making, from 1975 to 2005. The whole point had been to protect small investors from being gouged by Wall Street sharps. But just 3 years after its implementation in 2007, the Flash Crash proved it to be a disaster.

Endnotes

1. Edgar Ortega, "NYSE Loses Market Share and NASDAQ Isn't the Winner," *Bloomberg News*, June 24, 2009.

2. Thomas Peterffy, Chairman and CEO, Interactive Brokers Group, "Comments Before the General Assembly of the World Federation of Exchanges," October 11, 2010.

3. Dan Mathisson, "Unfair at Any Speed: Why Success Itself Is the True Target," *Traders Magazine* Online News, August 11, 2009.

4. Testimony of James A. Brigagliano, Co-Acting Director, Division of Trading and Markets, U.S. Securities and Exchange Commission. Concerning dark pools, flash orders, high-frequency trading, and other market structure issues, www.sec.gov/news/testimony/2009/ts102809jab.htm.

5. Senator Ted Kaufman, "Unusual Market Activity: The SEC and High-Frequency Trading," May 13, 2010, *The Huffington Post*.

6. Securities and Exchange Commission, 17 CFR Parts 200, 201, 230, 240, 242, 249, and 270 [Release No. 34-51808; File No. S7-10-04] RIN 3235-AJ18, Regulation NMS, page 19.

3

Screaming Headlines

Sergey Aleynikov, a thin, amicable, 40-year-old naturalized citizen from Russia with a Richard-the-Lionhearted beard, thick black eyebrows, and a full head of thick black hair, had a nasty surprise waiting for him at Newark, New Jersey's Liberty International Airport when he returned there from a job interview in Chicago on July 3, 2009. FBI agents were waiting at the gate to arrest him for the theft of a top-secret trading algorithm from his former employer, Goldman Sachs. Aleynikov had been vice president for equity strategy at the big Wall Street firm, specializing in "architecture and implementation of massively concurrent low-latency, highly available distributed systems in the areas of high-frequency trading (HFT) and telecom," according to a resume that was posted on LinkedIn, a professional networking Web site. He reportedly was paid $400,000 per year, a generous salary for someone at the VP level, but probably a mere sliver of the money that Goldman Sachs was earning from its HFT activity. Goldman Sachs told Bloomberg that HFT was merely 1% of its $45 billion in total revenues, a piddling $455 million. But skeptics believed the firm's various HFT businesses earned several billion dollars.

Goldman Sachs had perfected the system over a ten-year period after acquiring it along with Hull Trading Company in 1999 for $500 million.

Aleynikov had accepted a position with Teza Technologies LLC, cofounded by Misha Malyshev, a former trader at hedge fund Citadel

Investment Group LLC, which claimed that it was unaware of Aleynikov's alleged theft.

The arrest would have remained a minor affair had it not been for some provocative comments made at a bail hearing on Independence Day by U.S. Attorney Joseph Facciponte, who was pressing for U.S. District Court Magistrate Judge Kevin N. Fox to incarcerate Aleynikov as a flight risk.

"What the defendant is accused of having stolen from this investment bank...is their proprietary, high-quantity, high-volume trading platform with which they conduct all of their trades in all the major markets within the United States and other places...Because of the way this software interfaces with various markets and exchanges, the bank has raised the possibility that there is a danger that somebody who knew how to use this program could use it to manipulate the markets in unfair ways," Facciponte said.

Goldman Sachs was a badly tarnished institution in 2009 in the aftermath of the taxpayer bailout of Wall Street, and its reputation would sink even lower in 2010 with revelations that it had bet against the success of investments it had sold to its clients. The public was steamed in March 2009 when it learned that Goldman Sachs had finagled the government into bailing out counterparties involved in credit default swap deals with troubled insurance giant AIG, which was the recipient of more than $80 billion in taxpayer funds. The public was in an anti-Wall Street mood owing to the financial cataclysm caused by its investment bankers. It felt that Goldman Sachs should take a financial hit as a consequence of its high-risk investments and viewed it as a manipulative scheming firm with too much power in Washington, DC. Critics called it "Government Sachs." Banking expert Christopher Whalen described Goldman Sachs as "a political organization masquerading as an investment bank, and they're sitting at the table with the top people in government."[1]

So, people were inclined to think the worst of Goldman Sachs. When the prosecutor said that the software allegedly taken by

Aleynikov could be used to manipulate markets, people assumed that Goldman Sachs in fact was manipulating the markets.

One of the first purveyors of the conspiracy theory was Dan Ivandjiiski, a naturalized citizen from Bulgaria who wrote, along with several colleagues, a popular blog with a sensationalistic bent under the pseudonym "Tyler Durden" at the Zero hedge Web site.[2] Ivandjiiski and his compatriots regularly took outlandish, unsubstantiated swipes at Goldman Sachs, accusing it of outrageous practices, such as monitoring visitors to its corporate Web site so it could front-run them in the stock market.

Ivandjiiski had come to the newsletter business by a circuitous route. His fledgling career as an investment banker came to an abrupt end in 2008 when Financial Industry Regulatory Authority (FINRA) barred him from the securities industry for insider trading. He never admitted the charges, but he did consent to entry of FINRA's findings in the public record. His alleged sin was making a grand total of $780 on inside information that Hawaiian Holdings, Inc. had convinced several lenders to increase their lines of credit to Hawaiian Airlines. He hung on in the unregulated precincts of the market, becoming an analyst for a hedge fund, according to a 2009 profile in *New York Magazine*. Contemporaneously, he began blogging about what he knew about the markets and, more importantly for his readers, what he suspected. He zeroed in April 2009 on Goldman Sachs and its HFT operation, blasting it for allegedly making "flash trades," a questionable Wall Street practice until then unknown to the general public. Exchanges were allowing high-frequency traders an advanced look at their customer orders and giving the traders first crack at taking the opposite side of the trades. Goldman spokesman Ed Canaday got into several public spitting matches with Ivandjiiski in 2009, which only served to increase the size of the young blogger's audience. In the eyes of many of them, the Aleynikov affair validated their worst suspicions about the firm and their best opinions about Tyler Durden.

Ivandjiiski was a classic muckraker, a skill he no doubt learned at his father Krassimir's knee. The elder Ivandjiiski worked as a writer and an editor at *Bulgaria Confidential*, a tabloid known for its controversial investigative reporting.[3] The paper's Web site asserted that it constitutes "the only official entities, offering economic, political, journalistic, and social consultancy for Bulgaria and the entire Eastern-European region."

The site boasted, "We consist of professional experts specialized on all aspects of modern trends of transition within the post Eastern-Bloc countries. We have offices in Bulgaria, Poland, the Czech Republic, Malta, Russia, etc."

The incorrigible Durden followed up the Aleynikov story with a July 22 report on a public clash about high-frequency traders between two stock exchange executives that he had read about in *Traders Magazine*. At a May 2009 conference on market structure, William O'Brien, the CEO of the Direct Edge Exchange, reportedly came close to trading punches with Larry Leibowitz of the NYSE, who at the time was executive vice president and head of U.S. Execution and Global Technology. He later was elevated to the chief operating officer. The argument was on the propriety of Direct Edge's use of "flash orders" to attract high-frequency traders to the exchange. For a price, these traders got to look at all customer orders a full, half-second before the data was posted to the market. The NYSE offered no such inducement and was losing customers as a result of its stand. Leibowitz contended Direct Edge and four other exchanges selling similar services, including NASDAQ OMX Group Inc. and the BATS Exchange, had given one class of trader an unfair market advantage and disadvantaged customers by slowing their offers by half a second.

The New York Times saw this particular blog and ran a prominently placed story about it on July 24. The story also mentioned the arrest of Aleynikov, the former Goldman Sachs employee, and discussed other purported abuses of HFT, the sort of shenanigans alleged by Arnuk and Saluzzi, although the two traders were not mentioned.

Reporter Charles Duhigg wrote, "High-frequency traders often confound other investors by issuing and then canceling orders almost simultaneously. Loopholes in market rules give high-speed investors an early glance at how others are trading. And their computers can essentially bully slower investors into giving up profits—and then disappear before anyone knows they were there."

U.S. Senator Chuck Schumer of New York, a native of Staten Island, had the endearing quality found in many persons from that vibrant, densely populated corner of the world of being all elbows and mouth. In a city of 23 million strivers, there are few other ways to stand out. The truncheon-tongued Senator also was not publicity shy. Quite the opposite, he loved to bask in the limelight. When he was the center of attention, he barely could suppress his winning grin. Many a person who had been trampled by inadvertently standing between the Senator and a TV camera could attest to the sharp-edged politician's craving for attention. Schumer read the story in the *Times* and immediately went into publicity overdrive. He sent a letter to Securities and Exchange Commission (SEC) Chairman Mary Schapiro urging the agency to ban flash trading and shared it almost immediately with all the major media outlets.

"This kind of unfair access seriously compromises the integrity of our markets and creates a two-tiered system where a privileged group of insiders receives preferential treatment, depriving others of a fair price for their transactions. If allowed to continue, these practices will undermine the confidence of the ordinary investors and drive them away from our capital markets," Schumer wrote.

The New York Stock Exchange (NYSE) was one of Schumer's constituents and a large employer in Lower Manhattan. Direct Edge was across the Hudson River in Jersey City. In all likelihood, Senator Schumer had heard complaints about flash trades directly from the NYSE, one of his most generous campaign donors. In regulated industries, politically connected companies regularly pull political strings to prevent competitors from poaching market share.

The *Times* story and Schumer's letter incented other news organizations to take a close look at HFT. The scrutiny became so intense that a segment on HFT even ran on Comedy Central's *Daily Show*, with make-believe news correspondent Samantha Bee, dressed as a "cash cow," urging investors to try some HFT before it was banned by the regulators. The segment featured Irene Aldridge, who had written a book on the subject.

In short order, HFT became a derisive term. Comically, the industry tried to change its label. One practitioner told journalists that he preferred his firm to be called an "automated proprietary trading firm."

"There have been automated trading firms around since at least the early 1990s. They traded as much as possible with automation, but they also had traders on the floor with handheld computer terminals," he said.

In the midst of the journalistic feeding frenzy, it wasn't long before reporters discovered Arnuk and Saluzzi's white paper and launched the pair into the limelight.

Saluzzi was invited to discuss his findings on Bloomberg television, a cable business channel. The interview was apparently seen by somebody at the SEC, because shortly after the broadcast, Arnuk received an invitation from Henry Hu, chief of the SEC's Division of Risk, Strategy, and Financial Innovation, to visit Washington, DC with Saluzzi and address the SEC staff. This was exactly the audience that the two traders wanted to reach.

Saluzzi and Arnuk brought along a PowerPoint presentation and assumed that they would be addressing a small group of people. Much to their surprise, they were ushered into a heavily populated conference room. The audience included some of the agency's other division heads and some of its top PhD economists. Afterward, Hu invited the pair out to lunch for extended discussions.

In general, the regulators were intrigued with the two traders' thesis, but not everyone was convinced it was true. One questioner in the audience that day intimated that he felt Arnuk and Saluzzi's trading methods were flawed and that this was a more plausible explanation for their inability to hit the market's best posted price.[4] But most of the regulators did not dismiss them out-of-hand. Although the pair had no empirical evidence to prove their charges, they had raised intriguing questions that warranted further investigation. The economists welcomed their insights even though there was always the chance they would prove to be a "false positive"—which is computer-programming talk for a perceived problem that upon further investigation is proven not to exist. Arnuk and Saluzzi had made enough of an impression at the SEC with their market observations to excite its curiosity, however, which was no mean achievement. But they hadn't been able to convince the agency's staff members of the urgent need to roll up their sleeves and start making immediate adjustments to the market to head off a disaster.

Shortly after the meeting with the regulators, Arnuk blogged, "We take issue with a system where one type of participant is catered to at the expense of other stakeholders, unfairly. We take issue with order types and arrangements that favor and attract one type of player at the expense of other players. We would like a market where our regulators ensure that everyone has access to the same liquidity, no matter where their servers are located; we would like a market where one group is not shown another group's orders and intentions before they even hit the general marketplace. Is this not common sense?"

It may have been. But common sense about the markets was lacking among policy makers in the nation's capitol, save one man.

Endnotes

1. Marcus Baram, "Government Sachs: Goldman's Close Ties to Washington Arouse Envy, Raise Questions," *The Huffington Post*, June 9, 2009.

2. Joe Hagen, "The Dow Zero Insurgency," *New York Magazine*, September 27, 2009.

3. Ibid.

4. Author interview with SEC staff who attended the meeting.

4

Accidental Senator

The story in *The New York Times* caught the eye of another senator, a man who was more dogged and less of a showboat than Senator Schumer, whose efforts appeared to ebb a bit after the initial round of publicity. Ted Kaufman of Delaware was a newcomer to the Senate who appeared at first glance to be eminently worthy of obscurity. He had been appointed, not elected, to fill out the remaining 2 years of Senator Joe Biden's term after Biden was elected vice president. Kaufman was the last man you'd ever expect to emerge as a leading investor champion. But he did because of fortitude, emotional fire, and an uncommon knowledge of the Senate. His is truly a most remarkable political tale.

The septuagenarian Kaufman was clearly intended as a place-holder. Biden had made him promise that he would not campaign for the seat when the term expired at the end of 2010. The punditry concluded that Biden wanted an open seat so that his son Beau could run for it, establishing a Kennedy-style Democratic family dynasty in a state known to most persons for its nettlesome toll booth on Route 95, the East Coast's major highway corridor.

One would have expected a man of Kaufman's years to kick back and enjoy the ride, because his role obviously had been intended as ceremonial. He was selected, no doubt, because he was a long-time Biden loyalist and could be trusted to rubber-stamp the administration's controversial big-government agenda.

"If you can't have the original, go with the closest thing to it," said Delaware Governor Ruth Ann Minner when she named Kaufman to replace Biden 2 weeks after the November 2008 general election.[1]

Kaufman was an unusually gifted, experienced, and principled man—a placeholder whose constitution would never allow him to stand still. The tall, gentlemanly Kaufman knew more about the inner workings of Congress than most of its elected members. Kaufman had been Biden's chief of staff in the Senate for many years and was privy to all of the machinations of the chamber. He had other important qualifications as well. He possessed an MBA degree from the prestigious Wharton School of the University of Pennsylvania and an undergraduate degree in mechanical engineering from Duke University. He understood banking and finance, and he enjoyed fixing complex problems.

In 1966, at age 27, Kaufman moved to Wilmington, his birthplace, from Philadelphia to work for the DuPont Company. He grew interested in local politics—so much so that in 1972, he joined 29-year-old Joe Biden's long-shot U.S. Senate campaign against incumbent Republican Caleb Boggs as a volunteer in charge of voter turnout.

He began working full time for Biden in 1973 and 3 years later became Biden's chief of staff, staying with the Senator for 19 years. They became close friends, with Kaufman serving as Biden's right-hand man. Kaufman was thoughtful and level-headed. When Biden, in May of 1988, had surgery at Walter Reed Army Hospital in Washington, DC, for a brain aneurysm, Kaufman ran his office until he recovered.

Kaufman later became cochairman of Duke University's Center for the Study of Congress. He was running his own political consulting firm when Governor Minner asked him to take over Biden's Senate seat.

In appearance, Kaufman was closer to Abraham Lincoln than Biden. He was tall and lanky with a prominent brow, an unusually thin face, and warm and sympathetic eyes. If he had popped a stovepipe hat atop his bushy gray head and grown a beard, he would have made as convincing a Lincoln as Hollywood's Raymond Massey had in 1940.

After accepting Biden's seat, Kaufman asked to sit on both the Judiciary Committee and the Foreign Relations Committee. They had been Biden's committees and were the ones that Kaufman knew best. He should have requested a seat on the Banking Committee. He had been outraged by the greedy, risky practices of Wall Street that had devastated the economy with a "horrific" impact on American families. He wanted to do something about it—something that would ensure that Wall Street would never again commit such an outrage.

Equally angry with Wall Street was Jeffrey Connaughton, the gifted lawyer/lobbyist who Kaufman chose as chief of staff in December 2008. Connaughton, a dogged, passionate, driven man, reminded people of Roy Neary, the character played by Richard Dreyfuss in Steven Spielberg's classic *Close Encounters of the Third Kind*. He was disappointed that Kaufman had not sought a seat on the Banking Committee, which was hammering out historic legislation to reform Wall Street and the banking sector. Kaufman, however, did not believe he had the time to learn the ways of an entirely new committee and accomplish anything meaningful. He thought it more practical for him to work on the Wall Street problem through the Judiciary Committee. After a few months in office, he had convinced a number of his Senate colleagues serving on that committee, both Democrats and Republicans, to cosponsor the Fraud Enforcement and Recovery Act of 2009. The bipartisan bill authorized $160 million to hire FBI agents and prosecutors to prosecute the individuals who had perpetrated the massive mortgage fraud behind the country's economic collapse in 2007.

"The public needs to know that when mortgage brokers, or credit raters, or Wall Street bankers break the law, they'll be treated like the criminals they are. We can't have one set of rules for people who rob banks and another set of rules for banks that rob people," Kaufman said in a speech promoting the bill from the Senate floor. The bill was introduced on February 5, 2009 and swiftly passed both the Senate and the House by a wide margin. President Barack Obama signed it into law on May 20, 2009. It was quite an accomplishment for a placeholder and made him hungry to accomplish even more.

Kaufman and Connaughton both believed that Wall Street had to be re-regulated. In Kaufman's view, Wall Street had become as lawless as Dodge City during the Bush administration, which had considered overzealous regulators and heavy-handed regulation as impediments to growth, innovation, and profits. Kaufman was especially critical of former Congressman Christopher Cox of California, a Republican whom President George Bush had named as his Securities and Exchange Commission (SEC). Not only was Cox too hands off, in Kaufman's estimation, he had sinned by dismantling a regulation that had been put in place as a public safeguard following the Great Depression.

"I was just horrified at a whole series of things that they had done. One of them was their treatment of short selling. There's nothing wrong with short selling. I've done it myself," he said. But he was appalled that Cox had done away with the uptick rule, which made it more difficult to sell stocks short—and thus drive down prices when the market was in a free fall.

Cox and the commission had eliminated the Depression-era Uptick Rule in 2007, arguing that the regulation had been ineffective since 2001 when the stock market under pressure from President Bill Clinton's SEC Chairman Arthur Levitt had shifted from trading in eighths (12.5 cents) and sixteenths (6.25 cents) to decimals (1 cent). Under decimalization, an uptick of a mere penny would allow short-selling to begin. The rule had become obsolete, in Cox's estimation. The creators of inverse exchange-traded funds, which increased in value as the market dropped, added that the uptick rule had interfered with the returns on their new, popular products.

As soon as the rule disappeared, traders began engaging in a practice known as "naked" short selling, where speculators sold short stocks they didn't physically possess. Actual shares are supposed to be borrowed from other investors in a short-selling transaction and returned when the short seller closes out his position with a purchase, but some investors were bending the rules. With naked short selling, it was theoretically possible to short more shares than a particular company actually had outstanding. In effect, it was a license to print stock certificates.

This also was a violation of the law. The SEC could have sued them. Instead, Cox urged the SEC to revisit the rule and change the uptick requirement to a nickel. He said he had been misled about the efficacy of the rule by program traders and a trial run that had produced deceptive results about the efficacy of the Uptick Rule:

> "The elimination of the Uptick Rule was based on the heavy lobbying of the SEC by investors who engage in Quant or black box program trading techniques," said Cox. "The lobbying efforts suggested that the Uptick Rule interfered with the efficiencies in which their platforms executed trades and set forth a series of events that resulted in the elimination of the Uptick Rule. I offer that the SEC was fooled by the results of the pilot program on several fronts... Several economists suggested that the short sellers 'played nice' for the short term in order to achieve their longer term goals. But beyond that, and more germane to present policies up for determination, is the condition of the markets during the pilot program. The SEC never tested the elimination of the Uptick Rule during the market sentiments that derived the origination of the Uptick Rule in the first place—the bear market."

Instead of reinstituting the rule, however, the SEC opted for a temporary ban in short selling of 799 financial stocks. Members of Congress wanted to prevent short sellers from driving down the stock prices of weak banks that were beneficiaries of federal bailout dollars. In October 2009, when the ban expired, program traders again engaged in naked short selling. In fact, the market plunged the day after the temporary ban was lifted.

Connaughton came up with an idea for Kaufman to have a voice in reforming Wall Street even though he wasn't a member of the Banking Committee: He convinced Kaufman to pretend that he was a member over the next two years. They both understood the political process. They both understood that if Kaufman spoke publicly and repeatedly on targeted financial topics, he would develop traction in the press and on the Hill, regardless of his actual committee assignments.

They also felt the need to prod the SEC. They had a suspicion that it was a captive regulator, too deferential to the big investment houses and funds to take any independent action that might ruffle Wall Street feathers. So Senator Kaufman also would act like a shadow SEC chairman, cajoling the agency and its new chairman, Mary Schapiro, to get tough with Wall Street.

"And that's what we did. We developed the Kaufman 'brand.' Beholden to no one, he took on Wall Street on behalf of the average investor every day during his term in office. The press wanted to write that; and so his influence grew by getting into the weeks and giving repeated speeches and interviews," said Connaughton.[2]

Connaughton was born and raised in Huntsville, Alabama, in 1959 and attended the University of Alabama during famed-football coach Bear Bryant's golden era. Exceptionally bright and captivated by politics, he attended the 1978 meeting of the National Student Congress held at the University of Pennsylvania in Philadelphia. Senator Biden addressed the student gathering, and Connaughton was so impressed with the young lawmaker that he invited him to come speak at the University of Alabama. Biden subsequently appeared at the school on several occasions, including as a keynote speech at a National Student Congress meeting held there. At the conclusion of the meeting, Connaughton drove Biden to the airport and told him, "If you ever run for president, I'm going to be there."

After graduating with his bachelor's in 1981, Connaughton obtained an MBA from the University of Chicago in 1983 and worked in the public finance departments of Smith Barney and EF Hutton. When Biden ran for president in 1987, Connaughton left Hutton and joined the campaign staff in Washington, DC. On Connaughton's first day on the job, the DC staff put the new campaign worker on a train to Wilmington, Delaware, which sat two hours to the north, and said, "You are going to be working for Ted Kaufman."[3]

Biden lost, and Connaughton returned to Washington, DC with him to work as an aide on the Senate Judiciary Committee from 1987 to 1991. Bitten there by the law bug, Connaughton enrolled in Stanford University's law school and earned a JD in 1994. He accepted a clerkship with Ab Mikva, chief judge for the U.S. Court of Appeals. One month into his clerkship, President Bill Clinton selected Mikva to serve as White House counsel. Mikva brought Connaughton along as a special assistant counsel to the president. Connaughton worked in the White House for two years and then moved on to private practice. In 2000, he teamed up with another former White House lawyer named Jack Quinn and a Republican lawyer who was working for the Bush campaign named Ed Gillespie to cofound Quinn Gillespie & Associates, which quickly became one of the most powerful lobbying firms in the capital. Money came pouring in from eager clients. The trio later sold the company to advertising and marketing giant WPP and made a fortune. Connaughton had it made financially. Freed from the rat race, he pined to go back into public service. He had always wanted Joe Biden to be president. Now that Biden was VP, he would have liked to join his hero in the White House, but President Obama had prohibited persons who had been lobbyists in the previous two years from taking White House jobs. So Connaughton decided instead to serve Biden by assisting Kaufman.

"Abusive short selling is tantamount to fraud and market manipulation and must be stopped now!" Kaufman harangued from the Senate floor on the evening of March 16. He had a strong voice and the populist's gift for projecting outrage. He urged the SEC to reinstate the Uptick Rule. Critics like Kaufman blamed naked short selling for the precipitous drop in the share prices of major financial firms like Bear Stearns and Lehman Brothers in 2007 and 2008, claiming the bearish investors had helped sink the firms, wrecking the economy.

Kaufman stayed on point. In June 2009, he urged Obama's SEC Chairman Schapiro to crack down. In January 2007, 550 million shares failed to deliver. By January 2008, 1.1 billion shares failed to deliver, and in July 2008, more than 2 billion shares failed to deliver, he said. That meant that the short sellers had never owned a single one of the shares. "These fails-to-deliver drove stock value down further than the market would have done by diluting stocks' prices," he asserted.[4] He kept on the offensive. And he began to get powerful pushback from Wall Street from a contingent he did not recognize: high-frequency traders.

"We wondered why they cared so much," he said.[5] They had excited his curiosity.

Then came news of Aleynikov, the former Goldman Sachs trader, and the allegations by Senator Schumer about flash trading. Kaufman began to connect the dots and decided to immerse himself in the issues surrounding the arcane, murky world of high-frequency trading (HFT). He recognized that this sector of the market was wild and unregulated, and he was determined to force the regulators to shine a spotlight on it. Here was an opportunity to protect the public from another financial blowup. Lack of transparency and regulation in the credit default markets had contributed to the blowup that had brought down AIG and Bear Stearns and Lehman Brothers. Wall Street had taken huge, idiotic risks to get rich quick. Kaufman sensed that the same dynamic of fast money, lax regulation, and risk-taking was at play in the HFT corner of the market.

The SEC alarmed Kaufman, too. The agency seemed complacent about the big change in the stock market. He had discovered that it had virtually no data on HFT, nor did the agency seem remotely curious about it. Yet, according to the best available estimates, HFT firms were behind 50% to 70% of all equities trading. Their trading machines had taken over the market.

Kaufman compared the situation to a football game without referees: "Bad things will happen in the pileup," he said.[6]

The flash-trading controversy was his hook. He could climb the stump and wave his arms and get people worked up about it. The practice was patently unfair. Some traders were getting a look at customer orders before anyone else did. It created a two-tier market, and that was undemocratic. It was an issue that would excite the reporters.

"If people begin to believe that if they go into the U.S. market they will be front-run by high-frequency traders, then they won't go into our market at all," he thundered. And that, he'd added, would have dire consequences for the nation's future growth.[7]

Privately and publicly, Kaufman began pressing Schapiro to take action on HFT. He felt she needed a push. Otherwise, she'd probably put the issue on the back burner. She already had a full plate. Schapiro's SEC was focusing most of its attention on Capitol Hill where Massachusetts Democrat Barney Frank, chairman of the House Financial Services Committee, and Connecticut Democrat Chris Dodd, chairman of the Senate Banking Committee, were crafting legislation to reform the financial industry so that there'd never again be a credit market meltdown like the one that had just transpired. Schapiro spent a great deal of time peering over the shoulders of the two committee chairmen to defend the interests of the SEC. She was most afraid they might clip the agency's wings and transfer some of its authority to the Federal Reserve. In the end, the SEC would maintain its turf, but the historic legislation would end up saddling the SEC a to-do list containing more than 80 new chores, including studies and the adoption of new regulations, and a deadline of two years for most of them.

Simultaneously, Schapiro struggled to reinvigorate the agency, to make it more aggressive. The SEC had missed uncovering the Bernie Madoff Ponzi scheme because somnambulant bureaucrats had ignored direct complaints between 1992 and 2008. There had been a pair of half-hearted investigations and some cursory exams of Madoff's firm but, according to a report by the SEC's inspector general, "a thorough and competent investigation or examination was never performed." The episode had been a demoralizing embarrassment. Schapiro was trying to bring back the zeal and spirit that the agency had had at its inception. She recruited new blood, including Wall Street hands with trading backgrounds and other direct market experience. Kaufman said it was as if she was fighting a big fire and he walked over and said, "Look, there's another blaze staring on the other end of the block."

Schapiro was an old Washington, DC hand. She had finely tuned political antennae. Schumer, going to bat for the New York Stock Exchange (NYSE), had urged Schapiro in a public letter in July to ban flash trading. Kaufman was on her back too, riding under the banner of a man of the people. With the Wall Street reform bill in play, the SEC needed all of the friends on the Hill it could get. Two senators represented a great deal of fire power. Schapiro convinced her fellow commissioners to propose a flash-trading ban.

Schumer may have been placated. Kaufman wasn't. In a statement released on August 4, 2009, Kaufman placed his cards on the table. "I'm pleased that SEC Chairman Schapiro has said the Commission will soon move to ban flash orders. But that is not the end of the story. It is becoming increasingly clear that naked short selling was just the first of a series of issues surrounding the way stock trades are executed that create unfair advantages for powerful insiders," he said. "We seem to be learning more every day about certain order types, high-speed trading, collocation of servers at exchanges, dark pools, and other indications that we have a two-tiered market: one for privileged insiders with high-speed computers and another for the average investor who must follow the rules. We need the SEC to move with urgency to restore investor protections and thereby strengthen the credibility and integrity of America's financial markets," he said. In short, Kaufman wanted Schapiro to take the high-frequency traders head on.

Kaufman, whose Wall Street crusade, as predicted, had attracted a considerable following of journalists, used his bully pulpit in September 2009 to urge the SEC to conduct "a comprehensive, independent, zero-based regulatory review of a broad range of market structure issues," including HFT. The SEC had anticipated Kaufman and behind the scenes had already begun planning a review of the market to see if current rules were outdated. Kaufman's pressure had gotten the SEC to open its eyes. The agency now realized that in the three short years since 2007, when it had implemented Regulation NMS to increase the role of automation in equity trading, the technology may have gotten out of hand. Schapiro told Kaufman that the SEC was preparing to issue a "concept release" come January to request comments from the public on the wisdom of updating the regulations.

Reacting to the news, Kaufman wrote to Schapiro, "There are at least two questions that must be posed—questions we must look to the markets' regulators to answer. First, had these opaque, complex, increasingly sophisticated trading mechanisms been beneficial for retail investors, helping them to buy at the lowest possible price and sell at the highest praise with the lowest possible transaction costs, or have they left them as second-class investors, pushed aside by powerful trading companies able to take advantage of small but statistically and financially significant advantages? And second, do these high-tech practices and their ballooning daily volumes pose a systemic risk? To take just one example, is anyone examining the leverage these traders use in committing their capital in such huge daily volumes? What do we really know about the cumulative effect of all these changes on the stability of our capital markets?"

When the SEC published its concept release in January 2010, it specifically raised Kaufman's questions. The concept release also reflected agency concern about the allegations that Arnuk and Saluzzi made.

This relatively quick response was unusual for the SEC and tribute to Schapiro's decision some months earlier to create a new Division of Risk, Strategy, and Financial Innovation. She had populated it with economists and MBAs with real Wall Street experience and academics like Henry Hu of the University of Texas whose studies had focused on market risk. This was the first new division within the SEC since the Great Depression, and it was meant to inject the agency with some vigor. So Kaufman had made a difference. The SEC was going to shine a light on HFT. Yet Kaufman remained dissatisfied. The SEC tended to move slowly so that it could build a consensus among all market participants before acting. The concept release portended a process that could take as long as three years. And the result might be a compromise that avoided injured feelings but did not realistically correct the problems that HFT firms were creating.

Perhaps Schapiro was just trying to humor Kaufman, knowing he'd be leaving the Senate at the end of 2010. He wondered. In any event, Kaufman had a gut feeling that the SEC could not afford to wait so long to address the problem.

Kaufman had good reason to worry. Like indulgent parents, regulators often end up being controlled by their charges. Over the years, the SEC had been inordinately influenced by Wall Street's powerful interests. This had occurred for many years, not just during the term of Christopher Cox. Economist John Kenneth Galbraith sketched the dynamics of regulatory capture more than 50 years earlier: "Regulatory bodies, like people who comprise them, have a marked life cycle. In youth they are vigorous, aggressive, evangelistic, and even intolerant. Later they mellow, and in old age—after a matter of 10 or 15 years—they become, with some exceptions, either an arm of the industry they are regulating or senile."[8]

Kaufman and Schapiro met face-to-face for the first time in Kaufman's office in either late October or early November 2009. Kaufman was skeptical that she truly shared his concerns about HFT. He looked at her and said, "I don't think you are going to do anything."

She answered, "You just watch."

Endnotes

1. www.whorunsgov.com.

2. E-mail from Jeffrey Connaughton to the author, June 20, 2010.

3. E-mail from Connaughton, August 24, 2010.

4. Senator Ted Kaufman floor speech, June 24, 2009.

5. Author interview with Senator Ted Kaufman, September 8, 2010.

6. Jim McTague, "DC Current," *Barron's Magazine*, January 25, 2010.

7. Ibid.

8. John Kenneth Galbraith, *The Great Crash of 1929* (New York: Houghton Mifflin Harcourt, 2009), 166.

5

Flash Crash

Six months after her confrontation with Senator Kaufman, Chairman Shapiro faced one of the most dramatic stock market crashes in history. On Thursday, May 6, 2010, at 2:30 p.m., a massive trading anomaly dubbed the Flash Crash shook Wall Street like a magnitude-ten earthquake, shattering the weakened faith of small investors in the structural integrity and the fairness of the equity market. The event also shook up regulators. They had viewed the fears about high-frequency trading (HFT) and the potential for a rapid market meltdown expressed by persons like Kaufman and Arnuk and Saluzzi with skepticism. Now this lightning-quick market move—the fastest and deepest intraday rise and fall in history—proved in fact that something was seriously amiss with the decentralized, computer-dominated, equity market system created by the Securities and Exchange Commission (SEC) in 2005. Within a matter of minutes, stocks and futures markets fell a stunning 5%.[1] The Dow Jones Industrial Average skidded 998 points in about 10 minutes, wiping out $1 trillion in equity. Dozens of blue-chip stocks, long considered safe havens for investor nest-eggs, went into violent death spirals that in some instances took their share prices down 35% or more in 120 seconds. Exchange-traded funds (ETFs), sold to cautious investors on the basis of their mutual-fund-like attributes, fell like rocks. There was high-pitched panic in the trading rooms of brokerage firms and hedge funds. Investors were stampeding for the exits like cattle, and no one knew exactly why. Had a massive computer error started the mass of selling, just as Arnuk and Saluzzi had warned, or had some bad news from

Europe or the Gulf of Mexico come to light, news which had not yet
gotten to them?

Then just 10 minutes into the crisis, the market suddenly reversed
itself. The Dow Jones Industrial Average (DJIA) recovered in a
minute and a half. It was almost as if some benevolent wizard had
stepped onto Wall Street and waved his magic wand and restored the
market close to where it had started. Whipsawed investors were left
dizzy as drunks on a merry-go-round. A few appeared to have lost their
shirts. Others, mainly program traders whose computers provided
them with the wherewithal to act on such short notice, appeared to
have hit home runs.

By far the biggest cost that bizarre afternoon, however, was a loss
of the average investor's confidence in the integrity of the market.
The so-called little guy—the market's backbone—began to pull his
savings out of equities just as he had done in 2007 and 2008. This was
a potentially troubling sign for the economy. If retail investors sat on
the sidelines, corporations would find it more costly to raise new
equity, which ordinarily is a more attractive and less expensive form
of financing than debt. A similar episode of market abandonment had
happened in the past, with ugly economic consequences. Individual
investors had fled the markets in 1970 and 1971 after the speculative
Go-Go years of the 1960s ended in the failure of 129 white-shoe brokerage firms.[2] Some of the bankrupt companies had violated the law
by pledging customer securities as collateral for loans. This commin-
gling of funds threatened to wipe out about 40,000 small investors.[3]
Congress made these victims whole again by 1973 by pledging a $1
billion line of credit from the Treasury to a new federally chartered
insurance fund similar to the Federal Deposit Insurance Corporation
(FDIC) and by squeezing money from the surviving firms to capitalize this new entity. Congress dubbed the fund the Securities Industry
Protection Corporation, or SIPC. Even so, small investors did not
return to the equity market in meaningful numbers until 1983. In the
intervening period, both the economy and the markets had been

anemic. A dollar invested in the Standard & Poor's (S&P) 500 on January 1, 1970 would have yielded 86 cents on December 31, 1979.

The frightening extent of the psychological damage caused by the Flash Crash became evident by June 30, 2010, when the mutual fund industry reported its flow-of-funds data for the first 6 months of the year. Investors who had fled the markets in 2007 and 2008 had put $40 billion into equity funds from January 1 to the end of April 2010, according to the Investment Company Institute. That compared to an inflow of $5 billion for all of 2009. Following the Flash Crash in May, investors immediately yanked out $25 billion from equity funds.[4]

A market free fall was supposed to be a near impossibility. In 1988, securities regulators had put safeguards in place—so-called circuit breakers—to prevent wild swings like one that crashed the market over a number of hours on Black Monday 1987, when automated trading programs triggered massive sales of stocks. These were the market equivalent of a deep-sea oil rig's blow-out preventers. The circuit breakers worked imperfectly when the market fell suddenly again in 1989, so the SEC introduced a new, improved version in the early 1990s. A 10% drop in the market before 2 p.m. would result in a 60-minute trading halt. If the same percent drop occurred between 2 p.m. and 2:30 p.m., trading would be halted for 30 minutes. After 2:30 p.m., the market would have to fall a full 20% before action was taken. In this case, the market would be closed for the day.

Granted, the circuit breaker system was pretty long in the tooth by 2010, especially in light of a market structure whereby lightning-fast computing machines had replaced human traders. In place of men who once had come together to swap shares of stock on behalf of their customers stood row upon row of super computers. The computers were faster and more sophisticated than anything dreamed of in 1990. Small trades that had taken 10.1 seconds to execute in 2005 took 0.07 seconds by 2009. In 2010, some trades were being conducted in .002 seconds— 150 times faster than the blink of an eye, according to Commodities Futures Trading Commission (CFTC) Commissioner Scott O'Malia.[5]

As a consequence of the speed, volume on the New York Stock Exchange (NYSE) had increased by a whopping 79%.[6] That translated into an average daily volume of 5.9 billion shares, up from 2.1 billion in 2005. Average daily trades soared to 22.1 million versus 2.9 million in 2005. At the same time, the average trade size shrank, from 724 to 268.

Discussions on possible upgrades in the aged braking system had been underway at both the SEC and beginning in January 2010, albeit at a measured pace. There was no alarm among the regulators because the market decline had been orderly during the credit crunch of 2007 to 2008.[7] It had survived a real-world stress test. In the regulators' minds, then, the circuit-breaker discussion was about addressing potential problems, not a looming crisis.

Kaufman and others had expressed a sense of urgency. This was wasted on SEC, a guarded, plodding agency that was aware that the unintended consequences of its actions could disrupt the economy.

The SEC staff made it clear in the release that it hadn't yet picked sides, noting that the interests of short-term traders and long-term traders often were aligned. Clipping the wings of the high-frequency flock might inadvertently hurt the retail and institutional gaggle. Short-term traders, for instance, favored volatility because it created more trading opportunities for them. Volatility was anathema to long-term investors. Yet the SEC noted that the net effect of trading strategies used by the HFT firms appeared to dampen volatility. One problem with this line of reasoning was that the SEC didn't really know what those strategies were because they were closely guarded secrets. The agency's remarks on volatility seemed to be parroting an argument often used by HFT firms to justify their activities.

Cognizant of its data gap, the SEC was also weighing a requirement to demand significantly more information from both traders and institutional investors about their stock transactions so that the regulators could follow an "audit trail" and gauge whether markets manipulation or other abuses were taking place. Cost estimates for the system ran into the billions of dollars. The bottom line was, however, that absent such a tracking mechanism, the SEC, the market's primary regulator, would forever be flying in the dark.

The trading day on Thursday, May 6 had begun on a negative note, which was not unusual given that the bears had been dominant the first two days of the week and given that investors had been notably jumpy the week before. The DJIA had moved more than 100 points six out of the past seven trading sessions, and that the Dow had declined by 284 points on May 4 and May 5, according to the Associated Press. At the opening of the market, the major stock indexes were off 4% from Wednesday's close.

There was ample reason for investors to have the jitters if they were long on equities and sitting on gains. Pundits warned that rioting in Greece might sink Europe's economy and in the process drag down the fragile recovery in the United States, ushering in another steep stock market decline like the one in 2007. Just as their portfolios were recovering, the whirlwind in Europe might sink them again. Investors were on the knife's edge: Should they sit out the crisis or take their profits and run?

The rioting in Athens had been massive but fairly benign, with some bricks and bottles tossed at police by demonstrators. Then on May 5, the protest turned deadly. Some of the 50,000 to 100,000 protesters became as angry as nineteenth-century anarchists. They tossed Molotov cocktails through the plate glass windows of a bank and burned to death three employees, including a pregnant woman. And what was the reason for this bloodlust? The rioters objected to an austerity proposal being debated by their parliament so it could make good on bonds sold to EU banks. The country of just under 11 million people had become a welfare state par excellence, administered poorly by legions of pampered public employees. The retirement age was 61, which was risible in an era when men lived close to 80. Tax dodging was epidemic. The government had borrowed heavily to finance itself by issuing bonds backed by fraudulent income statements. As a consequence, Greece was deeply in the red. And the outraged citizens of the cradle of democracy rose up and began murdering one another because they wanted to protect their unsustainable way of life—their ill-gotten gains.

Greek government debt stood at EU E300 billion, an alarming 113.2% of its gross domestic product (GDP). Compare that to a ratio of government debt to GDP in the United States of 69.1%, which in itself is considered inordinately high. The Greek government had a deadline of May 19 to meet its obligations, and its leadership was doubtful that it would be able to settle up with its lenders without massive help from the EU. Other countries were not stumbling over one another to fill the collection basket. Frugal German workers especially were piqued. Why, they asked, should their tax dollars be used to bail out a bunch of high-living wastrels?

Stock markets had fallen, and the Euro had fallen to new lows against the dollar, which boded ill for U.S. exporters because their goods would be relatively more expensive than similar products from countries including Germany, Britain, and France.

The Greek parliament was doing its part, pushing for higher taxes, cuts in the salaries of public employees, and an increase in the retirement age of all Greek citizens from 61 to 63 by 2015. But the Greek people refused to bite the bullet and go along. There was great fear in world markets that Greek politicians would buckle and simply default on their debts, eroding the capital of European banks that held billions in Greek bonds. This in turn would make lenders reluctant to extend credit to extend more loans to other shaky European debtors such as Spain, Portugal, Italy, and Ireland, plunging those counties into financial turmoil.

There were additional uncertainties on the eve of the Flash Crash. Troubling news was emanating from Great Britain, yet another continental country with serious debt problems. Voters replaced Labour Prime Minister Gordon Brown with Conservative David Cameron, but they did not give Cameron's party a clear majority, casting doubt on his promised program of austerity, a program required to put the country back on sound economic footing.

Closer to home, in the Gulf of Mexico, estimates of the spillage from the badly damaged Deepwater Horizon drilling rig were increasing geometrically. Consequently, so were the estimates of the devastating damage it could inflict on the economies of Louisiana, Alabama, Mississippi, and Florida.

On Wednesday, May 5, officials from British Petroleum journeyed to Capitol Hill to give House and Senate members private briefings on the Gulf oil spill, a meeting that backfired. The oil executives revealed that the well might belch as many as 40,000 barrels of crude a day, which was eight times what U.S. government officials had been estimating up to that time. Members of Congress were enraged. By Thursday morning, some of them were demanding a blanket ban of offshore drilling. Their comments further roiled the market because the end result of any such work stoppage would be a steep rise both in unemployment and oil prices.

Newscasters were using a cliché—calling the spate of bad news "A Perfect Storm," a reference to Sebastian Junger's book about a 1991 Nor'easter that capsized a New England fishing boat in the Atlantic. The violent storm was the result of an unusual confluence of meteorological events. The bottom line was that the investment climate was highly unstable.

The world's financial markets reflected the uncertainty. In the United States, both the equities and futures markets spent the morning and early afternoon of May 6 in negative territory. The S&P Volatility Index (VIX) was up 31.7%, the fourth largest, single-day increase ever. Gold prices were up and Treasury yields were down, indicating a flight to quality.[8] The cost of buying protection in the credit default swaps market against the possible collapse of Greek bonds became progressively more expensive. Big institutional investors were bidding up the cost of such insurance. The increase in pricing coincided with a press conference by officials of the

European Central Bank at 8:30 a.m. in which they failed to mention a possible purchase of Greek bonds to prop up that nation, which news investors were hoping to hear.[9]

Between 9:30 a.m., when the U.S. market opened, and 2:00 p.m., the DJIA already had fallen 161 points to 10,712 or 1.5%, and the S&P had fallen 33 points to 1,145, or down 2.9%. Clearly, it was not an auspicious day to be long equities.

Market watchdogs at the SEC and CFTC viewed the initial sell-off as significant but not out of the ordinary.[10] Anecdotal evidence suggested that most of the sellers were from the retail segment of the market—the segment dominated by individual investors.[11] This crowd traditionally reacted impulsively in the face of breaking news. Michael Goldstein, a finance professor at Babson College in Welles-ley, Massachusetts, about 14 miles west of Boston, described the investors as "quick to pull out of the market if something moves against them and quick to jump back in because they are afraid to miss a market rise."[12] In short, they were tormented by those age-old demons: greed and fear.

Around 2 p.m., some hedge funds and fund managers, sensing a big down day, began selling S&P 500 E-Mini futures contract on the Commodities Mercantile Exchange (CME) to lock in their gains. So many of these managers and traders sold at the same moment that the contract price fell from 1,113 to 1,056 in 27 seconds. Profession-als call this effect *correlation*. When investors are moving lockstep, prices are subject to huge swings.

The S&P 500 E-Mini is the most popular futures contract in the world because it is one of the most affordable futures products. Investors agree to buy or sell the cash value of the S&P 500 Index at a specific date. The E-Mini contract is valued at 50 times the S&P 500 Index. On May 6, when the S&P 500 was at 1,100, a single E-Mini contract cost $55,000. Larger index futures contracts are priced at $250 times the S&P 500. CME offers a panoply of E-Mini products that allow investors to dabble in foreign currencies, precious metals, agricultural commodities, and equities at a relative bargain price compared to traditional futures.

One of the largest E-Mini sellers this day was the venerable Waddell & Reed Financial, Inc., Overland Park, Kansas, which had entered the securities business in 1937 in the wake of the Great Depression. The firm decided to hedge a $7 billion position in U.S. equities by selling short 75,000 E-Mini futures.[13] It used an off-the-shelf algorithm to feed shares into the market at a pace that would keep them at 9% of the E-Mini market's overall volume. The hedge was massive, worth a total of $4.1 billion.[14] Waddell & Reed had made similar trades earlier in the year with no outsized impact on the market. But this was no ordinary day. If high-frequency traders had somehow detected the huge order in the market, using their sophisticated algorithms, they might have tried to front-run the order, selling ahead of Waddell & Reed and figuratively adding tons of snow to the avalanche.

What Waddell & Reed could not possibly know that day was that buy-side liquidity in the E-Mini had fallen by 55%, from $6 billion to $2.65 billion, by the early afternoon. Buyers had begun moving to the sidelines. The volume appeared to be larger than it was because HFT firms using 15,000 accounts were trading E-Mini contracts back and forth, several thousand times a second, to generate rebates. In effect, this game of ping-pong created the very situation Arnuk and Saluzzi had warned of in their white paper—an appearance of deep liquidity where, in fact, it was thinner than spring ice. Waddell & Reed sold only half the order—35,000 contracts—as the market declined. But there were lots of other sellers, too. Altogether, they tried to unload 80,000 contracts during the same period. But there were only buyers for 50,000 contracts. That large imbalance between buyers and sellers sent prices rushing downward and triggered CME's stop logic functionality, pausing E-Mini trading for 5 seconds.

This halt in trading was a major market event. The commodities markets had experienced a Flash Crash–like episode earlier in the decade and had responded by creating the braking system designed to allow computerized traders to take a deep breath and assess the situation. Five seconds was a considerable pause in a world where program trading was dominant. It gave buyers time to appreciate that there was no fundamental reason for the steep E-Mini sell-off. There had been no bad surprises—at least yet—from Europe or anyplace else. When investors realized that fear, not fundamentals, had seized the market and that E-Mini contracts had been oversold and were at bargain-basement prices, they jumped back in and began buying. The E-Mini contract price began to recover. So did the prices of exchange traded funds (ETS), which had been propelled downward by the same overwrought anxieties. The crash had been halted at the CME. The day was not saved, however. Something totally unexpected occurred. The panic that had infected the commodities market leapt like wind-blown hot ash to equities exchanges and ignited a conflagration of panic selling.

How was this possible? How could an event in the commodities market impact the separate and distinct equities market? They were distinct trading venues. Each had its own rules and its own set of regulators. Each had distinct investment products. The answer was that the two markets had become virtually integrated because of the activities of the high-frequency traders and their super computers. The HFT firms had programmed their trading machines to look for pricing discrepancies, also known as *arbitrage opportunities*, between the two marketplaces and to trade the two markets simultaneously to exploit them. For instance, at times one or more of the individual stocks that make up the S&P 500 would rise or fall on the equities exchange, owing to earnings news, and the futures index would be relatively slow—milliseconds late—to adjust its price up or down to reflect the changed value of that individual stock component. The HFT's lightning-fast machine would buy the stock and short sell the future, betting that they would converge in price, which usually happened seconds later. So the HFT firm would make a profit on both of the trades—one in the equities market and one in the commodities market. Often it was mere pennies per share. But there were millions of these arbitrage opportunities every day to be exploited by the traders with the fastest computers.

On May 6, the E-Mini futures on the CME fell ahead of the individual equities over on the stock exchanges. After the 5-second pause was implemented on the CME, high-frequency trades that previously had sold E-Mini contracts or had stepped away from the market came back in as buyers because their algorithms predicted a rebound in prices. But their computers at the equity exchange sensed that the underlying stocks in the S&P 500 would fall in value, due to selling. The high-frequency traders began selling the underlying stocks. As a result, about 2:40 p.m., selling volume on the stock exchanges began to snowball (see Table 5.1). The downhill momentum was much stronger than the computer algorithms anticipated. One market maker's model predicted that the DJIA was on course to finish the day 5,000 points lower.[15] Many of the algorithms had instructions to liquidate all positions and exit the market in the event of unanticipated trading patterns. That's what many of the machines began to do, draining liquidity from the market. Sell volume was so unusually high that, absent the traders, the exchanges could not handle them all. There was so much message traffic that some of the exchanges were unable to acknowledge the receipt of buy and sell orders let alone locate buyers for the sudden surge of sellers.

TABLE 5.1   Summary of Major Index Moves: Lows from Previous May 5 Close (4:00 p.m.)

	S&P 500 Index	S&P 500 ETF	DJIA Index	E-Mini Futures
2:00	–1.78%	–1.81%	–1.51%	–1.78%
2:40	–4.35%	–4.45%	–3.91%	–4.43%
2:45–2:47	–8.58%	–10.12%	–9.16%	–9.18%
3:00	–4.90%	–5.05%	–5.00%	–5.12%
4:00	–3.30%	–3.37%	–3.26%	–3.48%

Source: SEC

"The data coming back from the exchanges was garbage," said one trader. In some instances, the information about trade volume and prices was 20 seconds old. Rather than risk making erroneous trades based on the faulty market data, these traders simply shut down their computers.[16]

Part of the problem was that the NYSE was upgrading quote systems for its listed stocks, and the work was only half done. So when a flood of sell orders came in and slowed the entire consolidated tape, data for the stocks that had not been upgraded lagged even more.

There was also some highly circumstantial evidence that some high-frequency traders deliberately had flooded the market with trades to slow down the consolidated tape.[17] These traders were among those who had the special feeds from the exchanges to their collocated servers that provided them with an advance peek at actual pricing data. The SEC, which in 2005 had eliminated provisions in the Securities and Exchange Act that prohibited the independent distribution of market data, believed the time advantage between the data delivered by the direct feeds and the data on the consolidated tape was somewhere in the neighborhood of a few milliseconds.

In fact, however, the time delay could be several seconds on a normal day, and the time differential on May 6 sometimes gave HFT firms a 35-second informational advantage. This evidence, later discounted by the regulators, suggested to many investors that the HFT firms had sold their open positions when they saw the retail customers were beginning to panic. The tape delay had given them a head start to the exit. Prior to May 6, these HFT firms deflected attacks on their activities with boasts that they brought added liquidity to the markets, narrowed the spread between the bid and the offer prices, and reduced volatility.

But this day, the HFT firms' actions contributed to the opposite outcome. As they withdrew, *liquidity*—the ability to quickly convert your equity into cash at a fair price—evaporated. Spreads widened. Volatility soared (see Figure 5.1). The only people left in the markets were panicked retail investors trying to protect profits they had realized since the first of the year. They ordered their brokers to sell. It was a mistake. Like the HFT firms, the brokers showed their true colors. They were not their customers' friend. The market was sinking, and it was every participant for himself. The brokers stopped automatic execution of customer orders, also known as *internalization*, which on most days accounts for nearly 100% of retail trades.

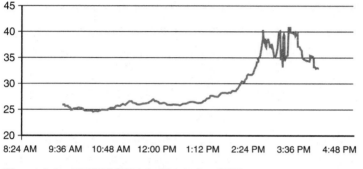

Figure 5.1   CBOE SPX Volatility Index (VIX).

Source: SEC and Bloomberg

When it was internalizing, a brokerage firm would try to match one of its customer's orders with that of another customer, in-house. The broker sweetened the deal by offering some price improvement over the national market price—usually amounting to a hundredth of a cent for each share. This was to comply with an SEC rule allowing internalization only if a customer receives a price equal to or better than the best bid and best offer displayed on the consolidated tape. If the firm could not make the trade, it sent the order to its executing broker, which gave the broker a legal kickback for the order flow. The big ones were Knight Capital, Citadel, and UBS. The executing broker would generally take the opposite side of the customer order because retail customers tend to buy high and sell low, making it exceedingly easy to make money off them from the spread.

Imagine a stock that is trading with a best bid and best offer of $15.55 by $15.85. An uninformed retail trader will either submit a market order, buying at $15.85, the full spread or put an order in at

$15.83, nearly the full spread, believing he is saving money. An informed trader, on the other hand, would be unwilling to pay the full spread and place a buy order much closer to the bid price of $15.55.[18]

In the rare instances when an executing broker demurred, it would forward the order to a dark pool, usually one owned by his firm. (*Dark pools* are electronic-trading venues where institutional investors trade stocks away from the public stock exchanges.) If the dark pool can't execute the trade, it is sent to one of the stock exchanges. This largely automated process occurs in subseconds.

On May, when the market fell out of bed, the internalizers reduced their executions of customer sell orders but continued to execute the buy orders. In other words, they'd sell stock to a retail customer but wouldn't buy stock from a retail customer. They wanted to get rid of their own inventories, not accumulate more shares. So they forwarded virtually all their customer sell orders onto the swamped stock exchanges.[19]

The damage to retail investors was substantial. Twenty thousand trades, totaling 5.5 million shares, were executed at a price 60% or more away from pre-Flash Crash price levels, and thus later were deemed invalid. At least half of those were retail orders. And, of course, that says nothing of the countless trades done at discounts of less than 60% but still large.

Between 2:30 p.m. and 2:40 p.m., the plunge in prices accelerated. Each of the major stock indices fell 5% or more in 10 minutes.[20] Sellers began to outnumber buyers geometrically because more and more buyers were disappearing. This was a major development because the HFT firms had replaced the old-fashioned human market makers and exchange trading floor "specialists" who had a legal obligation to buy or sell a particular share when no other party was willing to take either end of the trade.

The specialists also had a pecuniary incentive to trade—they could charge a fat spread. High-frequency traders had no obligation to make a market; they were not compensated to take such risks.

Some large players left the market anywhere from 5 minutes to 15 minutes, whereas others left for just 30 seconds. The bottom line was that stock prices fell like an avalanche because few people wanted them at that moment.[21]

Initially, the pickup in velocity was due to "stop loss" orders. These are like ejection seat buttons in a jet fighter. If the jet is falling to earth, the pilot ejects to save his life. Some investors place stop loss orders below the current price of a holding, to lock in a profit. Let's say the stock is at $30 and the investor paid $20 for it. If he's suddenly feeling bearish about the market, he could place a stop loss order to sell at the *market* if the securities price should drop to $28. A *market price* is the best price available at the time. If the investor is lucky, he'll get "stopped out" exactly at $28. But if there are no buyers for his shares at $28, he'll get the next best price, depending on his place in the queue. That could be $27.50 or maybe less.

Regulators later theorized that stop loss orders triggered a chain reaction. Then velocity picked up even more when something they never envisioned dragged stocks to ridiculously low depths. Traders, it seems, overlooked their "stub" quotes.

Under the SEC's rules, some market makers and exchange specialists were required to constantly post prices on both sides of the market for the securities they specialize in. A lazy man's method of complying with the annoying regulation was to post one bid price and one asked price so far out of the money that under normal circumstances, they never, ever would be "hit" by an actual trade. A buy order might be listed at a penny and a sell order at $10,000.

Most of the world, including a majority of Wall Street's regulators, didn't know what stub quotes were before the Flash Crash. The concept literally was off the radar. During the years that the SEC had been busy drafting rules to "improve" the market, its bureaucrats and more than 100 advisors from Wall Street had focused on possible new consequences of the regulatory changes. They hadn't thought to look in the closet at the old things like stub quotes and stop loss orders to see how the SEC's new rules might affect them.

On May 6, the avalanche of selling became so large and buyers, including specialists, so scarce that in some corners of the market, those ridiculous stub quotes were the best price that a seller could get.

Accenture, a global company with $22 billion in annual revenue, saw 66,277 of its shares trade down from $41.01 to a penny and back again between 2:40 p.m. and 2:46 p.m., a mere 6 seconds.[22]

A penny is better than nothing. According to the SEC, some 200 stock equity issues actually traded at 0, including stalwarts like Exelon, Boston Beer Company, and CenterPoint Energy.

ETFs fell particularly hard, with 160 issues falling 100% below their close on May 5.[23] ETFs—especially ones that mimic the action of the S&P 500 or some of the large market sectors—are extremely popular with traders trying to ride market momentum because, unlike mutual funds, they can be bought and sold like stock throughout the day. ETF's performance is linked to a specific basket of underlying stocks. The value of an ETF, then, depends on the value of those underlying securities.

The American Stock Exchange pioneered ETFs in 1993 with the introduction of one based on the S&P 500 Index, known as Spiders (Amex: SPY).[24] At the time of the crash, there were 985 ETF products for sale in the U.S. market, and investors had $797 billion riding on them.[25] They represented 30% of the total volume traded on national exchanges. Institutional investors were fond of using them as a cut-rate hedging tool. They could go long or short an entire sector using ETFs. An investor could, for instance, go long the dollar on the commodities markets, betting that the currency would strengthen, and hedge against being wrong by purchasing an ETF that invested in gold mines. When the dollar sinks, precious metal investments generally appreciate, and vice versa.

Retail investors saw ETFs as an attractive substitute for mutual funds because their management fees were lower and because they traded like stocks. There were ETFs that tracked the major indexes and others that focused on particular sectors such as energy. There were also ETFs that increased in value as the market declined—so-called "short" ETFs—which provided an inexpensive means of playing the short-sellers game. Of course, sector bets were risky. To guard against downside risk, retail investors relied on stop orders and limit orders as a means of bailing out if the market should go against them.[26] In effect, everyone would pile into the same lifeboat if the market began to sink.

On May 6, the individual stocks that made up the ETF baskets fell so rapidly that market makers struggled to value the ETFs accurately. Simultaneously, anxiety about potential trade cancellations due to the wild market action caused professional traders to back out of this segment of the market, too.[27] This sudden loss of liquidity caused the ETFs to fall even faster, which in turn triggered investor stop-loss orders, one right after the other. Once triggered, the orders became "market orders" to sell at the best available price, so downside momentum in the ETF sector increased because the market orders could find no buyers. It was like watching a long line of dominoes tumble (see Figure 5.2).

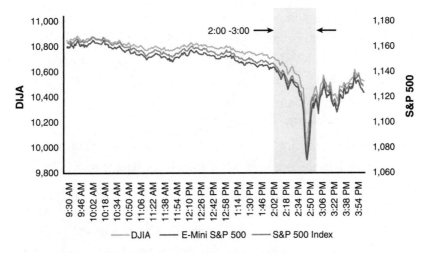

Figure 5.2   The securities markets on May 6, 2010.

Source: SEC

About 86% of all listed stocks fell less than 10% from where they had been priced at 2:40 p.m., which was by no means the sort of disaster that would drive an investor onto a window ledge. However, the remaining 14% of listed stocks—including some of the biggest names—fell much further, some by as much as 100%.

There was another major factor that contributed to the crash: In the equities market, there was no universal braking system like the CME's stop logic. Each exchange had its own fail-safe system. In the face of the crash, the NYSE instituted a trading slowdown for specific stocks that were falling rapidly. It described this tapping of the brakes as instituting a Liquidity Replenishment Point. In the acronym-mad world of securities regulation, it was known as an LRP. Once the LPR was triggered, human stock brokers on the floor took over from the machines and tried to right the buy-sell imbalance in the affected securities by the old-fashioned auction method of trading. The NYSE was the only U.S. equities exchange left with human floor brokers. And because they worked side by side with automated versions of themselves, it was known as a *hybrid market*.

In the old days, pre-2007, when the NYSE was the exchange with the lion's share of trading volume, a trading recess there could stop almost any selling stampede as effectively as that tiny aborigine boy, Nullah, stopped the panicked cattle from going off a cliff in the movie *Australia*. But the NYSE on May 6 was no longer king of the equities market. Panicked investors merely sidestepped that exchange and placed their orders on one of the other 70-plus trading venues that comprised the national market system. Over at the BATS Exchange—the acronym stands for Better Alternative Trading System—sell orders routed from other exchanges soared by 8,000%. In short, the investors ignored the outstretched arms of the NYSE and simply ran off the next nearest cliff. The NYSE later would report that prices at its exchange—also known as The Big Board—did not reach the ridiculous levels reported by competitors who had no braking mechanisms at all for chaotic conditions.

Ten minutes into the panic, with the DJIA down more than 700 points, the professional traders who had run from the market began to reassess the situation and come back in to buy. Ten minutes after their reentry, the market was up close to where it had begun—a breakneck trip of about 1,000 points in 20 minutes. There were some equally wild rises on the upside, with both Sotheby and Apple shares hitting $99,999 at one point, presumably because they hit stub quotes in the bid side of some trader's book.

The roller coaster ride had been frightening, especially for sellers who had lost the profits they had been trying to protect and then some. And the fear lingered for months. Individual investors remained highly concerned that the unusual volatility of May 6 could occur again and again. They distrusted the market's ability to execute their stop-loss orders fairly and effectively. They believed the market was rigged in favor of high-frequency traders. Also among the wounded were some outstanding companies whose stocks had been unfairly pummeled during the disturbing episode. The Flash Crash, they would discover to their chagrin, had reduced their market capitalizations, robbing investors and employees of millions of dollars that had been put aside for savings and retirement.

Endnotes

1. Report of the Staffs of the CFTC and SEC to the Joint Advisory Committee on Emerging Regulatory Issues, "Preliminary Findings Regarding the Market Events of May 6, 2010." Washington, DC (2010): 2.

2. David A. Loehwing, "Rx for Wall Street," *Barron's Magazine*, September 4, 1972.

3. John Brooks, *The Go-Go Years* (New York: Allworth Press, 1998), 315–342.

4. Tomoeh Murakami Tse, "Quarterly Investment Outlook: Economists Wary After Socks' Recent Slide," *The Washington Post* (July 11, 2010).

5. From the opening statement by O'Malia at the May 14, 2010 meeting of the CFTC Advisory Committee on Technology, which he chaired.

6. Securities and Exchange Commission, "Concept Release on Equity Market Structure," *Federal Register* 75, no. 13 (January 2010): 3594–3614.

7. Regulators in September 2008 temporarily curtailed short selling in 799 financial stocks when bankers and politicians charged that the short sellers were manipulating investor fears to drive down the value of their shares.

8. CFTC and SEC, "Preliminary Findings," 11.

9. Ibid, 13–14.

10. Ibid, 2.

11. Author interview with representatives of the NYSE and NASDAQ OMX.

12. Jim McTague, "Volatility Villains: You, Me, and the Flash Traders," *Barron's* (online and print), June 5, 2010.

13. Tom Lauricella and Scott Patterson, "Legacy of the Flash Crash: Enduring Worries of a Repeat," *The Wall Street Journal*, August 6, 2010.

14. CFTC and SEC, "Preliminary Findings," 3.

15. Prepared Statement of Noel Archard, managing director of product research and development iShares U.S.A. before the CFTC-SEC Joint Advisory Committee on Emerging Regulatory Issues, August 11, 2010.

16. Author interview with a trader.

17. Jim McTague, "Was the Flash Crash Rigged?," *Barron's Magazine*. August 30, 2010.

18. Author interview with Dennis Dick, CFA, Bright Trading LLC, Las Vegas, NV, October 13, 2010.

19. Report of the Staffs of the CFTC and SEC to the Joint Advisory Committee on Emerging Issues, "Findings Regarding the Market Events of May 6, 2010," 58.

20. CFTC and SEC, "Preliminary Findings," 18.

21. Author interview with NASDAQ OMX Chief Economist Frank Hathaway on August 4, 2010.

22. Prepared statement of Pamela J. Craig, chief financial officer, Accenture, before the Joint CFTC-SEC Advisory Committee on Emerging Regulatory Issues, August 11, 2010.

23. Ibid, 73.

24. Letter from Michael J. Ryan, Jr., executive vice president and general counsel of the American Stock Exchange to Jonathan G. Katz, secretary, U.S. Securities and Exchange Commission, October 28, 2002.

25. Noel Archard, managing director, Blackrock, prepared remarks for the CFTC-SEC Advisory Committee on Emerging Regulatory Issues, August 11, 2010.

26. Ibid.

27. Ibid.

6

Shock and Awe

When the May 6 trading day ended, total trading volume had reached 19.4 billion shares—2.2 times the average daily trading volume in the fourth quarter of 2009. New York Stock Exchange (NYSE)-listed stock volume was the second highest in history across all trading venues, whereas NASDAQ-listed stock trading in all venues hit a new record high. Investor confidence was shaken, and official Washington, DC, no fan of Wall Street, was roused to indignation.

President Obama summoned Treasury Secretary Timothy Geithner and White House Economic Advisor Larry Summers to the Oval Office at 3:15 p.m. to brief him on the situation. The President, who had been hammered in the press for poor generalship at the outset of the BP oil leak, obviously did not want to look lackadaisical in the face of Wall Street's latest outrage.

Congress, also cognizant of the public's dislike of Wall Street, owing to the massively expensive rescue of financial firms in 2008 and 2009, was quick with a vocal reaction to the equity market breakdown. Just hours after the Flash Crash on Thursday evening, Congressman Paul Kanjorski, a veteran Democrat from Pennsylvania who, coincidently, was facing a tough reelection in November, called in reporters to announce a special May 11 hearing by his Financial Services Subcommittee on Capital Markets, Insurance, and Government Sponsored Enterprises on the Flash Crash. (Kanjorski would be swept out of office the following November.)

"Yesterday's Flash Crash was incredibly startling," said Kanjorski in his press release. "Within a matter of minutes, we faced a market that seemed just as volatile as it did in the fall of 2008. We cannot allow technological problems, regulatory loopholes, or human blunders to spook the markets and cause panic. This is unacceptable. In this day and age and with the use of such complex technology, we should be able to make sure that our financial markets are effectively monitored and investors are protected. We were lucky that the market appears to have caught the error and quickly rebounded. The SEC must investigate this important issue."

A Senate subcommittee similarly attuned to the public's anti–Wall Street leanings scheduled a hearing two days after Representative Kanjorski's. Everyone wanted to finger a culprit because the market had failed dismally, if only for 20 minutes.

To placate the Congress, the White House, and the public, the Securities and Exchange Commission (SEC), which oversees the equity market, and the Commodities Futures Trading Commission CFTC, which oversees equity futures, assigned a joint advisory committee of experts, including former regulators and two Nobel-prize winning economists, and charged it with ferreting out the root cause of the Flash Crash. This was an ad hoc decision 5 days after the event. The committee had been intended to help resolve differences between the two agencies that historically had been unresolved—things like the margin treatment of investor portfolios that contained both equity and commodities products and the treatment of "mixed swaps," which would have an equity feature hedged by commodity like a currency future.

Following Black Monday in October 1987 when there had been a similarly extreme market break, with the Dow Jones Industrial Average (DJIA) falling 22% in one day, the largest one-day decline since the Great Depression, the Reagan administration quickly assembled The Brady Commission to look into the event. That panel was led by

Nicholas Brady, Reagan's Treasury Secretary. Regulators at the SEC and the CFTC decided to take a similar course.

"We had the paperwork ready. We said, 'This is the answer,'" recalled CFTC Commissioner Scott O'Malia.[1]

Additionally, the staffs of the two agencies cranked out an 80-page report on the Flash Crash by May 18—a period of 12 days. Amazingly, in that brief period of time, they ruled out market manipulation as a possible cause. The rapid down and up, it seemed, was primarily the product of several glitches such as stub quotes, stop-loss orders, and an absence of a unified braking mechanism in the equities market that could be remedied fairly quickly and painlessly with some new rules. It was a band-aid approach.

Congress didn't buy it. Some members acquainted with the work of Senator Kaufman saw a direct link between the Flash Crash and high-frequency traders. In his opening statement on May 11, Representative Kanjorski said, "In recent years, high-frequency trading has exploded. Barely a blip two decades ago when technology constraints and growth last crashed the markets, automated traders today move in only seconds and make up as much as two-thirds of daily trading volume. Their decisions to trade or not to trade can produce real consequences." Another Congressman at the hearing referred to high-frequency traders as parasites.

Regulators ended up breaking about 21,000 trades on May 6 that they said clearly were erroneous, including 7,000 stubs trades involving 200 separate securities (see Table 6.1).

The trades were 60% or more below the price posted before the Flash Crash. At least 50% of the broken trades were retail orders. The 60% threshold was the result of an arbitrary decision. More than 20,000 trades had fallen from 20% to 59% and were left to stand.

TABLE 6.1   Distribution of Lows from 2:40 to 3:00 p.m.

	Total # of Trades	Total Volume	Total Volume ($)
All trades	7,135,104	1,995,000,637	56,651,582,692
Losses	5,013,724	1,358,709,226	38,047,617,508
0% to –10%	4,912,125	1,324,448,213	37,383,122,363
–10% to –20%	63,890	22,171,745	522,444,343
–20 to –30%	12,923	4,077,881	85,328,519
–30% to –40%	6,112	2,317,245	30,461,333
–40% to –50%	2,519	767,393	9,641,261
–50% to –60%	1,682	472,624	8,334,944
–60% to –70%	1,056	370,920	4,328,898
–70% to –80%	798	292,061	2,245,851
–80% to –90%	1,109	237,259	1,152,480
–90% to –100%	11,510	3,553,885	557,516

Gray highlighting = broken trades
Source: CFTC-SEC 1

"How our market operated on May 6 is a cause for embarrassment for us and our entire industry," said William O'Brien, CEO of DirectEdge Holdings, LLC, a stock exchange.[2]

An embarrassment? The Flash Crash was much more that. It was a warning sign that the markets were seriously flawed. If the regulators and the exchanges treated it as a mere embarrassment, they were almost guarantying that a similar, perhaps more devastating version of the Flash Crash would occur in the future.

Endnotes

1. Author interview on September 10, 2010.
2. William O'Brien, "Opening Statement Before the Joint CFTC-SEC Advisory Committee on Emerging Regulatory Issues," June 22, 2010.

7

Poster Child

Accenture subsequently became the poster child for the unnerving market event, if you can imagine a corporation that specializes in consulting being able to exert a pull on your heartstrings. CFO Pamela J. Craig did, in fact, elicit pity when she testified in August of that year before a joint Commodities Futures Trading Commission-Securities and Exchange Commission (CFTC-SEC) panel of experts that was engaged in a protracted Flash Crash autopsy. She showed that although the event might have been short lived, its fiscal effects were not. The Flash Crash had damaged the pensions and incentive plans of Accenture's employees worldwide.

Craig was the ideal witness. The middle-aged, slight executive appeared nervous and vulnerable, and that engendered empathy from the panel's august members. Her voice quavered. Clearly, she was uncomfortable being the center of attention in a CFTC hearing room overpopulated with television crews, journalists, lobbyists, and regulators. And the thin Ms. Craig was the only female in the room wearing a sweater to protect her from the air-conditioning on a day when temperatures outside hovered oppressively near 90 degrees.

There was the aura of a refugee about her. Her auburn hair, which extended to the nape of her neck, was limp from the humidity outside that hung over the Capital City's great outdoors that day like a moist wool blanket. Her frame was stiff. She had something she wanted to say, but it was obvious she would have preferred a somewhat less public venue. Her apparent uneasiness made her statement much more compelling than it would have been from the lips of some loud, cock-sure CEO. She gave Accenture a face. And this helped her communicate the dramatic consequences for her company of the dramatic market disruption.

Craig began businesslike with a litany of the company's vital statistics. Accenture, she said with slight tremolo, was a global company with $22 billion in annual revenue, a market cap of $29 billion, and 190,000 employees worldwide, of whom 32,000 worked in the United States. She said that 25,000 of the current employees were stockholders, including 15,500 in the states.

She followed immediately with an opinion that was sobering: "We recognize that there is still not total clarity about what happened on May 6. We do understand that there seemingly was a perfect storm of economic news around the globe, a reduction in liquidity in many securities, unusual trading volumes, and some technology challenges. Based on what we have all witnessed in the markets that day and since then, there is *every reason* to expect that this can happen again."

No one contradicted her assertion. SEC Chairman Schapiro or CFTC Chairman Gary Gensler and the rest of the panel listened to her remarks respectfully, occasionally nodding in agreement.

Craig said that her company had a unique perspective on the trading events of May 6, given that its stock had sunk to a penny per share. She related that at 2:40 p.m. on that day of market infamy, Accenture shares trading on the New York Stock Exchange (NYSE) had gone from $41.01 to $38, a fall of 7%, in just a few seconds, triggering the exchange's now notorious Liquidity Replenishment Point (LRP).

This initial drop was strange, perhaps a symptom of the blind investor panic and the avalanche of selling it had unleashed. Accenture was a profitable enterprise with healthy cash flow and strong margins. More than 70% of the shares were held by institutions like pension funds and mutual funds with long-term investment horizons. About 20% of the shares were owned by current and former employees, persons who were unlikely to dump their holdings merely because the Greeks, out-of-sorts with a government-imposed austerity program for their spendthrift nation, were torching banks.

Craig related, "At that point the NYSE stopped its own electronic trading in our stock briefly to go into *slow mode* so that market makers on the floor of the NYSE could then line up an orderly matching of trades." During the transition from fast to slow, the stock stopped trading altogether for just one minute. During the initial 10 seconds of that 60-second halt, brokers with "a few small market orders totaling 10,400 shares" simply rerouted them to other exchanges. These end-around orders included 19 trades of 100 shares each, all of which were executed at a penny.[1]

There was nothing untoward in the brokers avoiding the trading halt on the NYSE and taking their customer orders elsewhere. Market rules allow brokers to "trade through" exchanges where they cannot get a response to an order to buy or to sell, even if the exchanges are displaying the best bid and asked prices. The rule was designed to keep the market from grinding to an abrupt halt every time an exchange or specialist experienced a technological glitch. Brokerage house trading machines were programmed to avoid such roadblocks. Regulators never thought through all the possible consequences of the trade-through rule because they simply did not comprehend the overall mechanics of the national market system that they had created. In point of fact, prior to the great market dislocation of 2007 through 2009, Washington's regulators seldom discoursed with Wall Street. The SEC had always relied on self-regulatory agencies like Financial Industry Regulatory Authority (FINRA) to ride herd on the exchanges. The SEC audited these self-regulatory agencies to ascertain that they were conducting inspections of the exchanges and member firms as well as monitoring the day-to-day market activity, but the SEC's staff for the most part didn't spend a lot of time in the market trenches and was surprisingly ignorant about the market system's inner workings.[2]

When the Flash Crash was over, many of the piglets who had dumped shares into its vortex began to squeal that they had been robbed by market hogs armed with better information and faster computers. But there had been no stickup. Not one erroneous trade had been executed. Those penny stub quotes were legitimate because at the time of the trades they had met the definition of a market order, which was "the best available price at the time of execution." As for those who profited on the upside by virtue of superior technology, the market now had some aspects of the game of golf, where the players with the priciest clubs made the best scores. However, with members of Congress calling for hearings, the exchanges felt in this particular instance, many of the trades were not "justifiable." This was a new legal concept in securities circles born on May 6 from the political imperative to do something and do it quickly. And so at approximately 8 p.m. that evening, the exchanges arbitrarily decided to bust 20,000 trades that had been executed at prices more than 60% away from where they had been quoted at 2:30 p.m. It was tough luck, then, for those who had bought or sold at 59% away from that price level. It was also tough luck for savvy traders who had bought Accenture at a penny, realizing it was a steal, and had quickly sold it when it climbed back above $30-per share. They were now left with a short sale. They had to go back into the market and buy Accenture so they could deliver it to the purchaser, and they ended up paying more for the stock than the amount for which they had sold it!

Accenture employees were also big losers. Following the crash, those employees who were granted compensation in the form of stock and those who were signed up for the company's stock-purchase plan began having second thoughts.

"After May 6, many shareholders were concerned about why our stock was affected versus other large cap companies. We believe this sentiment is consistent with concerns of retail investors," Craig said in her prepared statement. The translation was that the event, which was three-months-old on the day of her testimony, had impacted Accenture's ability to raise equity capital, even from its own employees. Investors researching the stock would find that its 52-week low had been set at either $17.74 or $16.40, depending on the source of the data.[3] It would make the stock appear pricier than it actually was. During the market swoon of 2007 through 2009, one of the worst bear markets in U.S. history, Accenture shares never had traded below $26. The Flash Crash had distorted that achievement.

Craig offered a solution to prevent future distortions. She suggested that the SEC draft rules for implementation of so-called individual stock circuit breakers across all markets on most stocks. If a stock fell by 5% or more in 5 minutes in any of the exchanges, all would be required to halt trading for 5 minutes until the buy-sell imbalance could be restored.

The regulators didn't disagree with Craig here either, because this was one of their favored quick fixes—a fix that was favored by the stock exchanges as well. The problem was that the imposition of market-wide circuit breakers was little more than window dressing to get the Congress off of the regulators' backs. Academic studies going back to at least the 1980s had cast doubt on the efficacy of the devices. In theory, if investors panicked and overreacted, a trading halt would give them time to digest new information while stopping the proverbial "falling knife" that no one wants to catch. Buyers who perceived overselling would step in and reverse the panic selling. In practice, circuit breakers caused even more panic because sellers in search of liquidity were denied it. They assumed that the outlook that had caused them to panic in the first place must be the correct one.

A former Wall Street executive said, "Circuit breakers are an SEC attempt to make a fix after the fact. The SEC will try to figure out what happened, put a rule in place, and then we'll have people trying to circumvent the rule."[4]

Both the SEC and the CFTC were avoiding the real problem: Their incessant meddling with the market over 30 years had introduced significant flaws into the system. They inadvertently had created an environment that allowed short-term traders to commandeer the market; and although the traders clearing brought advantages to the market, they had brought some significant disadvantages, too. The indexes moved so wildly between early morning and late afternoon that long-term investors felt like they were rolling dice in a casino as opposed to investing capital for the long run.

Endnotes

1. Prepared statement of Pamela J. Craig, chief financial officer, Accenture, before the Joint CFTC-SEC Advisory Committee on Emerging Regulatory Issues, August 11, 2010.

2. Author interviews with numerous former regulators and numerous long-time Wall Street professionals.

3. Craig cited $17.74 in testimony. The exchanges showed $16.64.

4. Author interview in August 2010.

8

Accident Investigation

The haste with which the regulators narrowed their investigatory focus was perplexing. The list of possible Flash Crash suspects was long enough to populate an Agatha Christie novel, yet the regulators had ruled many of them out after only a few days. One regulatory official who was privy to the deliberations of the Commodities Futures Trading Commission-Securities Exchange Commission (CFTC-SEC) Joint Advisory Committee had been shocked from day one of the investigation when two members opined before the panel's first meeting even took place that the cause of the Flash Crash never would be known. He thought they were being defeatist. He wondered if the committee would make an honest effort to get to the bottom of the crash. The emphasis in the preliminary report—that a perfect storm of negative news from Greece and elsewhere had been a major cause of the Flash Crash—struck the official as an easy out for the panel. It was a lame excuse not to follow up on other leads.

A cynical public didn't buy the early explanation either. Because of the speed and violence of the crash, they suspected high-frequency traders and their marvelous computing machines were at the bottom of it all and perhaps deliberately had crashed the market to cash in on short-selling strategies.

A high-frequency trader opined that this theory was popular because he and his colleagues were considered mysterious, and their role in the market was patently misunderstood. Additionally, the trader said, in the public's mind the high-frequency trading (HFT) industry had been lumped together with Goldman Sachs because of the Aleynikov case.[1] And Goldman Sachs symbolized all that was wrong with Wall Street.

"When Goldman Sachs was associated with high-frequency trading—well, that wasn't exactly the best PR for our industry," he said.

That was an understatement. A *Wall Street Journal*/NBC news poll released on May 13, 2010 found that Toyota, which at the time was battling allegations that a glitch in the computerized accelerator pedals used in some of its most popular automobile models had caused more than 50 deaths, had a public approval rating of 31%. Goldman Sachs, which had been accused by Congress of betting against the investments that it had sold to its clients, had an approval rating of just 4%.

High-frequency traders were not the only suspects in the aftermath of the crash. In the large and vocal corner of the Internet's "blogosphere" dedicated to investing, pundits surmised the cause had to be a so-called "fat finger" trade, an erroneous sell order of massive proportions by a hedge fund, brokerage firm, or institution that would have changed the direction of the market and caused computers programmed to trade on momentum to sell, sell, and sell. In fact, on the day of the Flash Crash, a false rumor had been circulating that the entire event had been caused by some stumblebum Citigroup trader.

Still others suspected skittish retail investors trading in exchange-traded funds (ETFs) suddenly had turned bearish and triggered the selling panic. Because ETFs represent broad segments of the market, the selling would have driven down all stocks.

Terrorism by malevolent foreign hackers even was suggested in some quarters. The House Committee on Homeland Security held an informal inquiry into this possibility and came up dry. The SEC saw no obvious evidence of terrorism or hacking, but it was reluctant to rule it out entirely because the agency hadn't reviewed any of the market trading data.

Despite the plethora of theories, no one had produced a smoking gun. Finding one would be a huge undertaking. The "crime scene" was immense, with evidence scattered far and wide across its length and breadth. The problem was analogous to one that the Federal Aviation Administration would face if a giant airliner slammed into a field, violently exploding on impact, hurling millions of pieces of wreckage in all directions. Crash investigators might need several years to find enough of the debris to piece together a useful facsimile of the aircraft.

Traders had bought and sold 19 billion shares on May 6, and it would likely take several months before the government's over-stretched regulators could sort through those transactions to establish a convincing chain of causality. A single day of data for high-frequency trades in a liquid market is the equivalent of 30 years of daily data in a natural market,[2] and as previously noted, HFTs dominated equity activity. They represented 2% of all market participants, yet they generated 70% or more of the volume. Many of the firms traded one to two million shares every day.

Further confounding the investigation, there was no distinct "ground zero" within the crash site to cordon off with yellow tape. At the time of the Flash Crash, there were 11 registered exchanges exclusively for stocks. Most of them were electronic and had server farms where high-frequency traders could collocate their own computers to cut down on the latency or time it takes to execute a trade. (The closer a computer is to a destination, the faster the data flies to and from that point.) Any one of the HFT firms or the exchanges or their big institutional and hedge fund clients could have initiated the crash.

But there were many more rooms in this mystery mansion. There were more than 70 *Alternative Trading Systems* (ATSs) that were registered as broker-dealers and matched orders of buyers and sellers for all sorts of securities. And there were 5 electronic communications networks (ECNs), which were essentially ATSs that elected to display their best buy and sell orders on the consolidated quote so all investors could see their quotes.[3] Thirty of the ATSs were so-called "dark pools" that did not trade in the "lit market" and thus did not display their quotes. Large institutions such as mutual funds and pension funds that want to sell large blocks of a particular stock—say 150,000 shares—would not want to put such a large order into the public market, where it would be displayed on the consolidated tape because the sudden appearance of such a huge supply would cause the price to drop sharply before it could unload all its shares.[4] Dark pools attempted to cross these big orders by finding other big traders or by breaking the big order into smaller ones and dribbling the shares into the market.

In the over-the-counter market, broker-dealers "internalized" trades, matching one customer's order with that of another customer. The buys and sells, which are not publicly disclosed to the market, represented 17.5% of the total shares traded in the National Market System.[5]

Not only were there many rooms in the mansion, there was an adjoining wing: the commodities market, where traders bought and sold equity options, futures, currency, energy, and precious metals futures. Fourteen designated Control Markets were in operation in the commodities marketplace on May 6. Six of them were selling products that were so tightly correlated to the equities market that price direction on the venues moved in virtual lockstep. At one time, the commodity exchanges were associated strictly with agricultural products like pork bellies and hard assets like gold and other precious metals. By 2010, they also were offering an array of equities products such as those based on major stock indices like the S&P 500 and the Dow Jones Industrial Average (DJIA). They also had begun trading ETFs, which offer the attributes of a mutual fund and the liquidity of common shares. ETFs had revolutionized investing by providing the retail customer with an affordable, highly liquid instrument linked to the markets for precious metals, commodities, and stock-index products.

In sum, unraveling all the trades in all the markets made on May 6 to paint a picture of the Flash Crash would be an enormous undertaking, even for someone with the best data and equipment. But the SEC had second-rate stuff.

Thus, absent some industry Deep Throat pointing regulators in a specific direction, the detective work that would be involved in solving the Flash Crash mystery appeared to be monumental.

Endnotes

1. Author interview in July 2010.

2. Michel M. Dacorogna, Ulrich Muller, Richard B. Olsen, and Olivier V. Pictet, *An Introduction to High-Frequency Trading* (London: Academic Press, 2001), 6.

3. Testimony of James A. Brigagliano, Co-Acting Director, Division of Trading and Markets, U.S. Securities and Exchange Commission, concerning dark pools, flash orders, high-frequency trading, and other market structure issues (www.sec.gov/news/testimony/2009/ts102809jab.htm).

4. Ibid.

5. Investment Company Institute, "Re: Concept Release on Equity Market Structure" (File No. S7-02-10), April 21, 2010: 14.

9

The Trouble with Mary—and Gary

The Securities and Exchange Commission (SEC) and Commodities Futures Trading Commission (CFTC) chiefs in charge of the Flash Crash investigation had a litany of strengths but also a cart full of heavy baggage that could affect its progress.

Mary Schapiro, the first female to head the SEC, had to live down her imperfect record while at the helm of Financial Industry Regulatory Authority (FINRA), the brokerage industry's self-regulatory agency. Two big scandals had broken on her watch—the Madoff Ponzi scheme and the alleged, $8 billion, R. Allen Stanford investment scam—and she had been faulted for not uncovering them. Gary Gensler, chairman of the CFTC, had opposed the regulation of the credit derivatives market while serving in the U.S, Treasury under Bill Clinton. Inadequate regulation of this market had been a major cause of the credit market meltdown from 2007 to 2008 that put seven million people out of work and required federal bailouts of major Wall Street banks and brokerage houses.

Schapiro had seen her salary rise from $2.1 million annually to $3 million during her tenure, and she received a severance package valued at $7.8 million upon leaving, giving some people the impression that the task of lining her own pockets had distracted her from the task of regulating her charges. Adeptly dealing with the Flash Crash was an opportunity for her to make up for past sins, both real and perceived. In fact, she had taken one exceptionally imaginative step upon arriving at the SEC to make sure a Madoff-style scandal never

again blindsided her: She had created a new division, the first since
the agency's founding in 1934. The Division of Risk, Strategy and
Financial Innovation was staffed with risk specialists, economists, and
even some physicists to anticipate threats to the markets posed by
new and existing investment activities and products. Schapiro
recruited University of Texas professor Henry Hu to head the division. A renaissance man with degrees in science and law, Hu in 1993
had written a forward-looking piece for the *Yale Law Review* predicting that big financial institutions would make significant mistakes
employing relatively new products called *derivatives*. This was 5
years before the blowup of Long Term Capital Management, a hedge
fund that had made interest rate bets using the exotic products and
15 years before insurer AIG would blow itself up dealing in the exotic
products. Part of Hu's thinking was that credit default swaps, which
decoupled loans from the actual lender, led to "empty creditor" situa-
tions, undermining what it meant to be a debt holder.

The SEC had been dominated by lawyers who were more interested in writing regulations than actually riding herd on the markets.
Economists had been second-class citizens—dishwashers as opposed
to cooks. The new division housed virtually every economist at the
SEC and placed them on equal footing with the lawyers.

Hu from time to time brought in outside lecturers to keep his
division up to speed. He had been the one to invite Arnuk and Saluzzi
to talk to the staff about high-frequency trading (HFT) in November
2009. The day of the Flash Crash, Clara Vega, an economist with
Federal Reserve Board, was at the SEC at the behest of Hu present-
ing a seminar on her paper, "Rise of the Machines: Algorithmic Trading in the Foreign Exchange Market." The paper found that
high-frequency traders reduce market volatility and provide liquidity
to the marker in times of stress.

Back in the 1990s, Gensler, a former Goldman Sachs trader, had
been one of a cadre of good old boys that included Alan Greenspan
and former Treasury Secretary Robert Rubin that had kept the CFTC

under Brooksley Born from regulating derivatives despite her repeated warnings that these instruments posed a systemic risk to the financial markets. They treated her disdainfully, as if she were a meddling do-gooder who didn't understand the workings of the financial markets. Born later received the John F. Kennedy Profiles in Courage award for her effort to alert the establishment to an impending disaster. The citation stated, "In the booming economic climate of the 1990s, Born battled other regulators in the Clinton Administration, skeptical members of Congress, and lobbyists over the regulation of derivatives, warning that unregulated financial contracts such as credit default swaps could pose grave dangers to the economy. Her efforts engendered fierce opposition from Wall Street and from Administration officials who believed deregulation was essential to the extraordinary economic growth that was then in full bloom. Her adversaries eventually passed legislation prohibiting the CFTC from any oversight of financial derivatives during her term."

Born was now a member of the joint advisory committee that Gensler cochaired with Schapiro. There was no possible way he could produce a credible report without her endorsement in light of this past.

Schapiro and Gensler shared a number of attributes: Both had keen intellects, both had an insatiable thirst for achievement, and both were savvy political animals. They understood the importance of cultivating allies in the Congress, and they knew how to navigate the Capital's maze of bureaucratic and political back-channels, which was essential for accomplishing anything in Washington, DC. They were multi-millionaires as well and enjoyed the independence of mind and the insulation from pecuniary pressure that comes with that status.

Gensler earned his millions at Goldman Sachs, where he made partner at age 30 in 1988 in a class that included Lloyd Blankfein, who would rise to chairman and become the poster boy for everything that was wrong with Wall Street; John Thain, the last chairman of Merrill Lynch, who was ridiculed for spending $1.22 million to redecorate his office even as the firm was accepting a taxpayer bailout; and Bob Steel, the banking wunderkind who merged a troubled Wachovia National Bank with Wells Fargo and afterward served as deputy director for development for New York City for his friend Mayor Michael Bloomberg. Gensler started out trading currencies and bonds; moved into investment banking, where he specialized in media deals; moved to the desk that traded collateralized mortgage obligations; and ended up as cohead of the firm's worldwide finances, with 500 employees under his control. The Baltimore native had been a major Democratic Party fundraiser and advisor for financial policy issues. He advised Senator Paul Sarbanes in 2002 on what became known as the Sarbanes-Oxley Act, a sweeping corporate reform bill passed in the wake of the Enron, Tyco, and WorldCom accounting scandals. He enjoyed being a policy shaper and craved a more active role in politics, a wish that he shared with fellow Democrats.

In June 1997, President Bill Clinton made his wish come true. He named Gensler the assistant secretary for financial markets at the U.S. Treasury. Robert Rubin, another Goldman Sachs alumnus, was Treasury Secretary at the time. He served his masters well. In 1999, Gensler was promoted to undersecretary.

Gensler served until the end of the Clinton administration. When he left, he went to work for a venture capital firm and wrote a provocative book on the perils of mutual fund investing. But he retained his political ambition. When Hillary Clinton made a run for her party's presidential nomination in 2008, Gensler became her chief fundraiser. When she lost, he joined the Obama campaign and later became head of the president-elect's SEC transition team.

President-elect Obama named Gensler CFTC chairman in December 2008. But the appointment was not a slam dunk. A Senate floor vote on the nomination in March 2009 was blocked by Bernie Sanders of Vermont, a socialist who most often votes with the Democrats. Senator Sanders was steamed about Gensler's opposition to regulation of the collateralized debt securities (CDS) market all those years ago. He stated, "At this moment in our history, we need an independent leader who will help create a new culture in the financial marketplace and move us away from the greed, recklessness, and illegal behavior which has caused so much harm to our economy." The implication was that Gensler was not that man.

Gensler and the Obama administration genuflected before Sanders, promising to seek tough regulation of the credit default swaps marketplace. In a further concession to the New England senator, Gensler regulated both hedge funds and the energy markets to ensure that no one was manipulating the prices of heating oil and crude oil. Sanders lifted his hold on Gensler in May 2009. "The commitments I received from Mr. Gensler along with President Obama's strong plan to regulate financial markets demonstrate the administration's determination to make sure that the financial mess that we are in never happens again," Sanders said.

Gensler claimed he had learned his lesson and would be a tough, sensible regulator. He put it in writing. With the Flash Crash, he had an opportunity to deliver.

Schapiro, also a gifted climber, made her millions directly from her political service and connections. Other bureaucrats had parlayed their public service into fat paychecks, but few had succeeded as swiftly and as spectacularly as Schapiro had. Her first job out of law school in 1980 was trial attorney with the CFTC. Smart and eager, she quickly rose to the position of counsel and executive assistant to Chairman Susan Phillips. Phillips later would be appointed to the Federal Reserve's Board of Governors.

It didn't take Schapiro long to exploit her government service. In 1984, she left the CFTC for a fatter paycheck at the Futures Industry Association of America, where she worked as a lobbyist. The association's long-time president, John Damgard, had strong GOP connections. He had been an advance man in Richard Nixon's successful presidential campaign in 1968 and later became an assistant to Vice President Spiro Agnew. In 1988, Damgard used his connections to get Schapiro, a registered independent and 33 years old at the time, appointed by President Ronald Reagan to one of two Democratic seats on the SEC. She was reappointed to the seat in 1989 by Reagan's successor, President George Herbert Walker Bush. Schapiro served credibly. She wasn't a visionary or an innovator, but she knew how to build consensus.

Clinton named her acting chairman of the SEC in 1993. Later that same year, he named her Chairman of the Commodity Futures Trading Commission, where she served until 1996. She left there to become president of the national Association of Securities dealers, the self-regulatory arm of the NASDAQ stock market, and was named CEO in 2007. The New York Stock Exchange (NYSE) also had a self-regulatory arm. Both exchanges had different rules for its members, and the two regimes had become burdensome in an era when the NYSE issues could change on NASDAQ. Schapiro pursued the merger of NASD with NYSE Market Regulation, which produced FINRA in 2007. As a result of the merger, her annual compensation rose 57%, from $1,999,731 to $3,140,826. This was a sore point for the brokerage firms that had been NASD members. They felt Schapiro had enriched herself at their expense.

As an inducement to get member firms to approve the merger deal that created FINRA, Schapiro told the NASD members that they would receive checks based on the projected future savings that the merger was expected to generate. In proxy material sent to the members in December 2006, NASD claimed that the IRS was precluding it from paying them more than $35,000 each.

A lawsuit filed against FINRA by a California brokerage firm objecting to the small payout alleged that Schapiro and her staff had lied in the proxy material about the IRS ruling. It claimed to have seen a letter from the IRS that placed no such cap on the distribution, which came from $2 billion in members' equity that had been amassed as a result of the listing of NASD's NASDAQ market between 2001 and 2006. The suit claimed that the member firms had been entitled to $70,000 to $112,000 each.

The suit was dismissed in March 2010 when U.S. District Judge Jed Rakoff for the Southern District of New York ruled that self-regulatory organizations like FINRA and their officers are immune from private damages suits challenging "official conduct performed within the scope of their regulatory functions." But he did not rule on the merits of the case. Simply put, the way the law was written, even if FINRA had lied on the proxy and had short-changed its members, it was bullet proof. Protesting members had no recourse in a court of law.

Schapiro's reputation suffered as a consequence of the suit. Her $7 million package upon leaving FINRA didn't help matters, especially because critics had accused her of being a lax regulator.

Her priority at the SEC had been rebuilding the agency's morale, which was at a low after the Madoff scandal revealed severe shortcomings in its enforcement branch and dealing with the aftermath of the 2007 credit debacle. The Dodd-Frank financial reform bill required the SEC to implement 90 new rules in 18 months. The rulemaking process required that the agency post its proposed rules, accept comments from the public, and then redraft the rules to reflect sensible suggestions. She also had embarked on a review of market structure; the process that Senator Kaufman wanted speeded up because of the distortions caused by the high-frequency traders.

Now the Flash Crash had been added to that full plate. But just as it was for Gensler, it was Schapiro's golden opportunity to provide a better ending for the story historians would write about her.

10

The Road to Ruin

The history of U.S. investors and their experiences in the equities market has all the earmarks of an abusive relationship, and it would require an eminent psychiatrist several hundred pages to explain why battered investors return to the market time after time following their previous drubbing, knowing in their hearts that they eventually will be brutalized again.

Congress and the regulators, realizing the important role that small investors play in providing capital for American businesses, keep trying to save the marriage by imposing new rules on Wall Street. The rules work for awhile. But Wall Street always finds new ways in which to smack his spouse around, right under the regulators' noses.

Many of the complaints heard in 2010 about certain classes of traders having an unfair advantage had been voiced countless times in the past. Small investors always seemed to be getting fleeced by some Wall Street sharpie. The old Fred Schwed saw, *Where Are the Customer's Yachts?*, resonated as loudly with investors in 2010 as it did when he first published his classic Wall Street book of the same title in 1940.[1]

The particular thrashing that engendered the sweeping market reforms of 2005 took place in 1969 and 1970 when a stock market bubble burst and the consequent bear market slashed into Wall Street's brokerage profits, exposing the undercapitalized positions of more than 100 brokerage firms.[2] This massive collapse of so-called "white shoe" firms marked the first significant catastrophe for Wall Street since the Great Depression, and it was a wakeup call for Congress that the New York Stock Exchange (NYSE) and its regulator, the Securities and Exchange Commission (SEC), were not on the ball.[3]

The capital crisis was part of a one-two punch. The first punch was an embarrassing paperwork fiasco in 1968. Brokerage houses were overwhelmed by an unexpected influx of new customers at the zenith of a stock market bubble. The newcomers, expecting to get rich quickly, invested heavily in smaller, highly speculative stocks. The enthusiastic crowd drove trading volume to record highs, and the back rooms of the brokerage houses, where trades were settled manually, simply could not keep up with the flood of paperwork.

Failed trades—instances in which a transaction was voided because the seller's broker wasn't able to deliver an actual stock certificate to a buyer's broker—topped $3.47 billion by May of that year. The paperwork fiasco was so bad that many firms could not account for all the investor assets that were supposed to be in their safe keeping. Audits later would discover that some of the assets had been misallocated to collateralize the bank borrowings of several brokerage firms. In other instances, the securities simply had vanished, most likely into the pockets of dishonest employees. Frightened and disgusted, the public abandoned the market as quickly as it had embraced it at the height of the buying frenzy.

The SEC attributed the record-keeping disaster to brokerage firms that had hired stock salesmen instead of additional clerks when new customers, cash in hand, began pouring through their front doors. The pile of paper generated by this new business was so deep that the exchanges elected to halt trading every Wednesday to give the back-office grunts at the brokerages time to dig out from under the morass of customer orders.[4]

Not all the new customers were retail greenhorns. During the 1960s, institutional investors began to trade heavily on the NYSE, recalled Harvey A. Rowen, who was a lawyer at the SEC at the time.[5]

Most of the institutional clients were mutual funds. But they were joined for the first time by big bank trust departments and major pension plans that previously had thought stock investing would violate the "Prudent Man Law" designed to keep them from speculating.

"It dawned on them that they were really in violation of the law if they didn't buy stocks because stocks kept pace with inflation and bonds didn't," Rowen said.

Beginning in 1965, inflation became a major economic problem because of the escalation of the Vietnam War coupled with massive increases in federal spending for domestic programs.

"So all of a sudden there was this influx of trading in the New York Stock Exchange, which did 95% of the equity trading in the United States in those days. The member firms couldn't keep up because after a trade they had to clear the trades physically by delivering engraved pieces of paper called stock certificates to the other side of the transaction," said Rowen.[6]

The back-office paper-shufflers eventually began to make progress, but at a pace so slow it hardly satisfied the customers. SEC Chairman Hamer Budge noted in 1969, "At the beginning of the year, fails to deliver by New York Stock Exchange members totaled $4.5 billion. That figure represented 16.4% of the entire assets of member firms at the time. As of the third week in November 1969, fails were approximately $1.8 billion, representing roughly 6.5% of the assets of New York Stock Exchange firms." These fails in many instances were liabilities because the firms could not account for their customers' securities.

Despite the improvement, which saw service going from worse to merely bad, Budge reported that customer complaints about lost securities and botched transactions rose from 2,600 in fiscal year 1967 to 12,500 in fiscal year 1969.

"I should also mention that we have good reason to believe that the brokerage firms are receiving as many as 25 or 30 complaints for every one received by the commission," he said.[7]

In early 1969, Wall Street was struck by a bear market that was destined to last 19 months, reducing commission income at the firms and reducing the value of securities that they held in inventory. A tax increase in 1968 to reduce the budget deficit, followed in 1969 by fiscal restraint aimed at slowing inflation caused by the Vietnam War, slowed the economic expansion and triggered the mighty sell-off. As trading activity declined, resulting in lower revenues up and down Wall Street, brokerage firms began to quickly burn through their capital. The conditions of these big brokerage houses became so dire that market officials feared the sector might be wiped out by mass withdrawals of cash and assets by frightened customers. The NYSE had to intervene at 200 member firms, using a $25 million Special Trust Fund to make customers whole. More than 129 of those firms failed or were merged with stronger partners.[8]

Regulators taxed the NYSE with establishing capital standards for member firms and auditing them for compliance. The crisis in 1969 showed the standards to be ridiculously lax and the auditing process as practically nonexistent. What was worse, the NYSE relaxed the existing lax standards in the midst of the crisis, hoping to buy some time for troubled firms. The SEC didn't dare protest, fearing that if it did, the NYSE might not use its $25 million Special Trust Fund to reimburse member firm customers.[9]

The Trust Fund had its origin in the 1964 failure of the respected brokerage firm Ira Haupt & Co. The firm had been the victim of a $150 million soybean oil swindle run by a New Jersey commodities trader. Customers of the firm panicked, and there was fear that this panic would spread to the customers of other brokerage houses. The NYSE quickly had found a merger partner to buy the business, which helped calm the investors' nerves. But the NYSE's brand name had been tarnished, and the Exchange felt it had to take steps to burnish it. So with considerable fanfare, the exchange established the Special Trust Fund, promising to use it to restore the lost holdings of customers if another of its vaunted member firms were to fail.

This was no small sack of potatoes in 1964. Even so, it wasn't nearly enough to cover all of the customers affected by the serial brokerage firm of collapses in 1969. When the trust fund ran out of money, there still remained more than 40,000 brokerage house customers with empty pockets.[10] The exchange raised an additional $75 million through special assessments, and by 1972 all those poor souls had had their lost assets replaced. But this in itself did little to restore investor confidence in the stock market, which was evidenced in the share prices of publicly traded brokerage firms. These securities traded at a modest five- to- eight-times earnings, far too low for them to attract needed equity infusions.[11]

The NYSE begged the Congress to lend a hand to the markets by chartering an insurance system for the brokerage industry that would stave off runs at the surviving firms. The envisioned Securities Investor Protection Corporation (SIPC) would insure customer accounts up to $50,000 in the event their assets went missing when a member brokerage firm failed.[12] The new guarantor would have the implicit backing of the federal government.

It was not an easy sell in Washington, DC, or on Wall Street. Brokerages chafed at the prospect of paying annual premiums into the fund. Congress blanched at the recommendation that SIPC have access to a $1 billion line of credit from the U.S. Treasury. Authorizing legislation passed in 1970 by a narrow margin amid bickering and rancor not dissimilar to that seen in Congress in 2008 when it was called to bail out Wall Street again, albeit at considerably higher cost to the taxpayers. Congress insisted that SIPC be used for future crises only and demanded that Wall Street clean up its current mess *sans* government largesse. The exchange kicked in another $65 billion on a contingency basis to assuage the Congress.

SIPC notwithstanding, it was a long time before Wall Street's black eye began to fade. The Dow Jones Industrial Average (DJIA) had been at 955 in November 1968 at the peak of the investing frenzy. A year later, it stood at 700, and small investors were licking their wounds. The market recovered and broke 1,000 by November 1972, but small investors had sat out the rally, loathe ever again to trust in the market after their scalding three years earlier. Small investors, blinded by greed, eagerly believed the Wall Street sharps who told them they could get rich quick buying stocks—and they were utterly shocked to learn that they had been deceived.

Retail investors also had been frightened and disillusioned by the discovery that the strength of the brokerage firms to which they had entrusted their savings did not extend beyond the granite facades into their actual businesses. Worse for the titans of Wall Street, these investors felt that the deck was stacked against them in favor of institutions with access to superior research, better prices, and inside information.[13]

In large part, this feeling of being disadvantaged was the result of the absence of a consolidated tape. When an investor executed a trade in the 1960s and early 1970s, he had no clue if the specialist at the exchange was giving him the best available price or if a better deal was available in the same stock at one of the regional exchanges. The small investor always had inferior information.

"Dominant markets held pricing data close to the vest and wielded it like a club in competition with other markets," recalled former SEC Chairman Levitt. "Connections between markets were primitive or even nonexistent, making it virtually impossible to access better prices in other markets—that is, if you knew they were there. In the words of Congress, investor confidence was 'sagging.'"[14]

The small-investor boycott of the markets was evident in the data. In April 1972, the ratio of trades of 200 shares and less to the total volume of the NYSE was 50% of what it had been in 1968.[15] Investors had pulled money out of mutual funds for 14 consecutive months.

Absent the liquidity provided by the small investor, financial institutions concentrated their investments in large, international growth stocks, which quickly became known as "religion stocks"—stocks investors believed had enough liquidity to behave in a stable fashion. The lack of interest in other stocks caused an increase in volatility among them, characterized by abrupt, wild price swings and wide spreads.

This is eerily similar to the situation at the time of the Flash Crash in May 2010 when about 70% of all trading volume was concentrated in the shares of the 1,500 largest issuers. These large stocks had the narrowest trading spreads—as low as a penny. Stocks outside of this band had spreads ranging from a dime to a dollar or more.

G. Bradford Cook, who was the SEC's chairman in 1973, said, "In a sense we have a vicious circle: Without the orders of the individual investor, the market lacks liquidity, a situation that leads institutions to concentrate on the most liquid stocks, those with the largest number of shares outstanding. Of course, this concentration reduces liquidity as well as resulting in sharp price movements when institutions buy and sell. These price swings and the steady decline in prices of smaller companies in themselves discourage the individual investor and further aggravate the situation."[16]

Trading volume on the NYSE was down 9%. On the American Stock Exchange, whose listings were comprised almost exclusively of small growth companies, volume slumped by an astonishing 40%.

In retrospect, the real irony of SIPC was that it created an unanticipated consequence for the NYSE: It opened the door for Congressional meddling in the equities market. The meddling, in turn, led to the NYSE's dramatic loss of market leadership.

Endnotes

1. Schwed related a story about a visitor to the financial district who was shown the yachts of bankers and brokers at anchor in the Battery. "But where are the customer's yachts?" the innocent asked.

2. "Wall Street: Setting a Deadline for Reform," *Time*. September 11, 1972. www.time.com/printout/0,8816,906357,00.html.

3. A Flash Crash in May 1962, which saw the DJIA plunge 9% in 12 minutes, was shrugged off by most investors as an anomaly. Some saw it as a buying opportunity in the midst of a bull market. There was no serious attempt to discover what had caused the odd swoon.

4. John Brooks, *The Go-Go Years* (New York: Allworth Press, 1998), 182–187.

5. Interview with the author, August 26, 2010.

6. Ibid.

7. SEC Chairman Hamer Budge, Speech to the Investment Bankers Association of America, Boca Raton, December 9, 1969.

8. David A. Loehwing, "Rx for Wall Street," *Barron's Magazine*, September 4, 1972.

9. Ibid.

10. Brooks, 350.

11. Budge, Dec. 9, 1969.

12. Loehwing.

13. G. Bradford Cook, Chairman of the Securities and Exchange Commission, "Democracy in the Markets," an address to the Economic Club of Chicago, April 25, 1973.

14. Arthur Levitt, Speech by the SEC Chairman, "The National Market System: A Vision That Endures," Stanford University, January 8, 2001.

15. Ibid.

16. Ibid.

11

Busted!

The 1970 fiasco on Wall Street reverberated along Pennsylvania Avenue in Washington, DC, riling one of the most civic-minded, incorruptible, unassuming persons ever to occupy a seat in Congress—Representative John E. Moss of California. If you've never heard of him, you're forgiven. He's one of those great, influential, historical figures who slip between the cracks. Perhaps it's because he lacked flamboyance and was somewhat of a grind. When Moss passed away in 1997, the *New York Times* led its obituary with this left-handed compliment: "For a man who was variously described as dull, grave, quiet, humorless, hard-working, and plodding, Mr. Moss, a Democrat, left a surprisingly eye-catching legislative legacy."[1]

A profile in the *Wall Street Journal* described Moss as having "the righteous air and pompous tones of a self-important preacher." He rattled witnesses with a disconcerting stare.[2]

Moss's greatest legislative achievement was passage of his Freedom of Information Act (FOIA) in 1966 and passage of amendments in 1975 that gave the Act more muscle. For this feat alone, he is worthy of a statue. A doggedly determined man, he refused to quit or roll over, no matter how much pressure was brought to bear on him. He fought for passage of FOIA beginning in 1955 when he chaired a three-member subcommittee investigating the federal government's handling and distribution of information. Moss had discovered that bureaucrats regularly stamped even the most innocuous documents "classified" or "top secret." He was furious that this faux secrecy precluded taxpayers from holding bureaucrats accountable for their actions. Moss quixotically kept up the effort to gain more public access to government documents for 11 years until he could attract enough support for the measure, arguing that open government would protect freedom and prevent the government from sliding into dictatorship. Members of his Democratic Party were a major obstacle. He did an end-around by convincing a handful of Republicans to back the measure—including a young GOP lawmaker from Illinois named Donald Rumsfeld.

Moss's aide Michael Lemov recalled years later, "Virtually every executive branch department testified against the bill before the Moss subcommittee, asserting it would cripple the operations of federal agencies if they could not operate in secret when they deemed it appropriate."[3]

President Lyndon Johnson grudgingly signed the bill into law on July 4, 1966.

Moss's contribution to the Securities Amendments of 1975 was another game changer, providing regulators with a blueprint that they rely on even today. In retrospect, it may have been a law that should never have been passed, because it gave bureaucrats too much power to shape the markets, which was exactly the opposite of what he had intended.

Moss was an unlikely architect. He was not from a banking family, had never run a company, and was not wealthy. He did not have a college education. He was impelled by zeal to protect the ordinary citizen from abuse by the powerful. This populism reflected his own hardscrabble upbringing—a trial that would have ground most men to dust. Lemov writes that when Moss's mother and sister died one right after the other in Sacramento in 1927, his father simply abandoned him and his brother in a hay loft.

Moss exhibited his legendary scrappiness early on, fending for himself and his brother through the Great Depression. He took whatever job came his way. He sold tires, stocked store shelves, and even drove a hearse. Like many people who suffered during that era, he was close with his pennies, but in his case it was due to a charitable bent. Lemov relates that Moss walked miles to Sacramento Community College to save the dime bus fare so he could feed his brother.[4]

Moss wanted to change the harsh world in which he found himself, so he began to take an interest in politics. Inspired by Franklin D. Roosevelt's New Deal, he became active in local politics. The advent of World War II put his political ambitions on hold. He served in the Navy and then opened an appliance store when he returned to support his wife and their two daughters. The political itch remained. In 1949, he ran for a seat in the California State Assembly and won. He served two terms. He was elected to Congress in 1952 by a margin of four-tenths of a percent. Over the next 26 years, Moss proved to be a principled crusader who often exacerbated members of his own party as much as he exacerbated the Republicans.

In 1972, his House subcommittee's report on the state of the markets was the first independent examination of Wall Street since the Great Depression. Congress had demanded such a study after establishment of the Securities Investor Protection Corporation (SIPC). The lawmakers wanted to determine the exact causes of the Wall Street collapse two years earlier and to draw up a legislative plan to prevent it from ever happening again. The last thing the Congress wanted was for SIPC to be forced to draw on that $1 billion line of credit.

Moss's subcommittee drafted legislation that recommended a host of evolutionary changes on Wall Street intended to create a consolidated national market once the computer technology became available. In his view, computers would play an ever-larger role in trading and record keeping going forward. Computers in 1969 had made it possible for the United States to land men on the moon, so there was no reason that the marvelous machines could not be used to improve the efficiency of the U.S. stock market. Moss also wanted to see greater competition among the New York Stock Exchange

(NYSE), the American Stock Exchange (AMEX), the NASDAQ, and the regional exchanges, and he believed that computers eventually would become sophisticated enough to forge linkages that would give investors better access to all of them. As farsighted as Moss was, neither he nor anyone else anticipated that computers would morph into powerful desk-top PCs that would enable tech-savvy traders to take over the markets. In fact, the first hearing by the subcommittee focused on the back-office problems because this is what had generated the SIPC legislation. Computer processing of trades was viewed as the ultimate solution.

The first witness of that first hearing was Roger Birk, who ran the back office at Merrill Lynch. He rose to become CEO of the brokerage firm in 1980.

"We were talking about settlement in stock certificates—nitty-gritty kind of stuff—and we were learning how the NYSE really operated," said Rowen, who in 1971 had left the SEC to join Moss's staff. "And the more we learned, the more unhappy John Moss became, because the place was really a monopoly. It had Rule 394 that said if you were an exchange member, then you had to bring all your trades to its floor even if there was a better price someplace else, like at a regional exchange. The NYSE's commissions were fixed by the stock exchange staffs. They were not subject to competition among the member firms. The more we got into it, the more Moss wanted to do something about it," he recalled.[5] Moss became fixated on creating competition for the NYSE's order flow from regional stock exchanges and from over-the-counter market makers.

"And what came out of that whole thing was this requirement that the SEC was to create this system which would take advantage of existing technology and future technology as it developed and could automatically send the order flow to the place where the customer got the best execution. This was genesis of the National Market System," said Rowen.

In fact, once the envisioned central market system became a reality, the NYSE would be forced to rescind Rule 394. Big Board specialists would then have to compete head to head with their counterparts on the regional exchanges.

As Moss and the subcommittee drafted their bill, he repeatedly emphasized market competition.

"In the securities industry, undue emphasis has been placed on regulation instead of competition. We find the emphasis has been unwarranted, he said."[6] Rules had given the NYSE a virtual monopoly. Every last one of those protectionist measures in time would be stripped way.

The bill's drafters also envisioned a national clearing and settlement system to avoid repeats of the 1969 paperwork nightmare. Moss's original intent was to eliminate paper certificates altogether and rely solely on electronic registration. But he could not attract enough votes to add this provision to the bill. The American Banknote Company, which made its money producing these exquisitely engraved pieces of paper, had a great deal of political clout and was able to block the proposal. So Moss recommended creation of a Depository Trust and Clearing Corporation in which certificates would be deposited in a person's account and settlements could be conducted electronically from one account to another, just as in a bank.

Moss and the Congress also gave more money and power to the Securities and Exchange Commission (SEC). The NYSE and other exchanges would have to get SEC approval for any new rules. That had never been required before. Even so, Moss favored self-regulation. The stock exchanges would continue to police the activities of their members. Moss had wanted to give the self-regulatory authority to the National Association of Securities Dealers (NASD), but the NYSE complained about this usurpation to its allies in Congress; and Moss capitulated because it turned out that the NASD, which policed the NASDAQ over-the-counter market, wasn't interested in an expanded role.

The intended spirit of the 1975 law was captured in a speech 26 years later by SEC Chairman Levitt: "It is a vision rooted not in orthodoxy, but rather, in a practical recognition that investors are best served when diverse markets—exchanges, dealers, and alternative markets—compete for business; a vision where the best prices in any market are visible and accessible to all; a vision that embraces him the goals of competition, transparency, market connectivity, and best execution, but is mindful of the unheard tensions among them... The SEC's objective or function is not to dictate a particular market model, but rather, to allow the natural interplay of market forces to shape markets according to the demands of investors. Put another way, the commission has been charged by Congress to facilitate the development of a national market system. And this begins by providing the catalyst for market infrastructure refinements that serve the investing public."[7]

The one proposal in the 1975 law with the most immediate, beneficial, and revolutionary impact for investors was Moss's demand for an end to fixed commission charges at the exchanges.

Fixed commissions had been a way for the exchanges to ensure specialists and brokers a comfortable lifestyle, replete with the proverbial yachts. The stock-buying frenzy of 1967 and 1968, which had swelled customer rolls and had engendered an explosion in volume, minted more than a few millionaire stock brokers on Wall Street. About 50% of a brokerage house's revenue was from securities commission income, and the fixed charges exceeded execution costs by a handsome margin.[8] Customers viewed the rate structure as price fixing. It cost the same commission-per-share to buy or sell 100,000 shares as it did to buy or sell 100 shares. Some customers were inflamed by the practice of the exchanges of providing large institutional traders with expensive research at no cost in return for their business. They felt that the perquisite was paid in part by their high commissions. There were a number of lawsuits, including one that went all the way to the Supreme Court. The high court ruled that

customers could bring antitrust actions against the exchanges to challenge their commission structures. The Exchanges claimed they only
were able to provide all their customers, both big and small, with a
high-end service because of the inflexible price regime. They may
have been able to ride out the customer protests for years had not
Moss dragged Congress into the fight. The SEC, sensitive to its over-
seers, jumped on the bandwagon and tried to nudge the exchanges to
voluntarily abandon the practice.

The handwriting was on the wall in big block letters: Congress
wanted the change. In the Senate, New Jersey Democrat Harrison
"Pete" Williams was working on similar legislation. Unlike the dog-
matic Moss, he was willing to compromise with the industry, but not
much. Yet the brokers and the exchanges were blithely blind to the
message these lawmakers were sending them. They resisted every
effort to change their lucrative pricing scheme, arguing that a price
reduction would destroy the business, causing the failure of quality
brokerage houses and perhaps even the NYSE itself. The brokerage
industry already was limping as a result of the events of 1969—the
market swoon and the collapse of so many firms. There were 25%
fewer NYSE member brokerage firms with public customers, yet
their gross revenues were down by 25% in 1974 from 1972.[9]

Regulators pointed out that some large institutions already were
taking some business elsewhere to avoid the high rates. A so-called
"upstairs" market had developed where institutions traded big blocks
of stock directly with one another to save on brokerage fees, the precursor of "dark pool" trading venues. Other institutions cut deals with
regional exchanges.

The regulators were concerned that these practices were dispers-
ing order flow to multiple venues, some that were away from the
exchanges and thus opaque, and making it more difficult for retail
investors to obtain the best price on either a buy or a sell order. The
SEC in 1968 had convinced the exchanges to grant volume discounts.
With some more arm-twisting, fixed rates were eliminated in 1971 on

orders greater than $500,000 and, in 1972, on orders exceeding $300,000. In 1973, they were eliminated for orders less than $2,000. Remarkably, when the SEC asked the exchanges to voluntarily eliminate all fixed charges in 1975, all but one exchange refused. This was sheer pique. Fortunately, William Casey, who was chairman of the SEC at the time, was more realistic. A champion of business, Casey, who would go on to become the director of the Central Intelligence Agency, issued a report in 1972 calling for specific changes that would create the sort of national stock system dreamed of by Moss and Williams. This probably kept the lawmakers from introducing even harsher measures out of anger and frustration with the intractable club men of Wall Street. It may be why Moss allowed in his legislation for the exchanges to maintain a regime of self-regulation, overseen by the SEC, albeit more strictly than before. The industry claimed this self-policing mechanism would make the market more amenable to competition and innovation than would a high-powered federal bureaucracy, like an enhanced SEC. Casey, who often repeated his belief that the United States had the best system of capital allocation in the world and that it should be preserved, never objected.[10]

The SEC eliminated the fixed commissions on May 1, 1975, a day that the brokers began referring to as "Mayday"—after the distress call.

The impact of this particular change was radical and immediate. In September 1975, a former investment newsletter publisher named Charles Schwab opened the doors to a new kind of brokerage firm— one that offered steep trading discounts to small investors. Imitators soon followed. Schwab was perceived as a champion of small investors, and the opening of his discount service marked the beginning of the gradual return of their return to the market.

President Gerald Ford signed the Moss-inspired Securities Act Amendments of 1975 into law in June of that year.[11] Ford noted that the law contained a goof that would allow for the imposition of state and local taxes on security transactions; and he pledged to sign a technical corrections bill as soon as it reached his desk. But in retrospect, it had two other big goofs as well. The biggest goof in the act was that it gave the regulators too much discretion in the creation of a national market. Owing to his previous experience with bureaucrats stamping everything top secret to guard their turf from outside scrutiny and interference, Moss should have appreciated that they were obsessed with guarding their power and authority. The SEC would prove to be no different from any other bureaucracy. The SEC's approach to shaping the market would be heavy handed, with layer upon layer of complicating rules. Had Moss lived to see it, he would have regretted giving the SEC such a free hand.

The other goof was that the act granted entirely too many concessions to the NYSE, codifying a system of specialists in a way that would result in market fragmentation, not the intended, integrated national market system.

"The dealer problem has been aggravated by the fact that many specialists have neither the capital nor the inclination to handle effectively the large orders that come in from institutions, and thus this function has gravitated to large, well-capitalized firms who combined the broker and the dealer function by finding the other side for these orders to the extent possible, positioning the balance if necessary," noted SEC Commissioner Philip A. Loomis after passage of the measure. These well-capitalized firms constituted the so-called "upstairs market."

"Some restrictions prevent these firms from fully competing with the specialists, and prevent them from fully competing with him, thus preserving an uneasy balance. Thus, we do not have the national market system yet," Loomis said. However, he argued that owing to the impetus provided by the legislation, a national market system was inevitable.

"I believe we should get there as soon as possible," said Loomis. But he was wrong about the impetus. The NYSE was an obstacle to modernization. It would be another 20 years before the SEC began the process that would fully implement the 1975 Act.[12] And this would occur only because of another market disaster—Black Monday, 1987—a precursor of the Flash Crash.

Endnotes

1. Robert McG. Thomas Jr., "John E. Moss, 84, Is Dead; Father of Anti-Secrecy Law," *New York Times*, December 6, 1997.

2. Carol H. Falk, "The Investors' Friends," *The Wall Street Journal*, August 17, 1972.

3. Michael R. Lemov, "John Moss and the Battle for Freedom of Information 41 Years Later," Nieman Watchdog, www.niemanwatchdog.org/index.cfm?fuseaction= background.view&backgroundid=00191, July 3, 2007.

4. Ibid.

5. Author interview.

6. David A. Loehwing, "Rx for Wall Street," *Barron's Magazine*, September 4, 1972.

7. Arthur Levitt, Speech by the SEC Chairman, "The National Market System: A Vision That Endures," January 8, 2001.

8. SEC Commissioner A.A. Sommers, Jr., "Thoughts on Approaching May Day," a speech to the University of California Securities Regulation Institute, January 9, 1975.

9. Ibid.

10. Wayne E. Green, "Casey at the Bat," *The Wall Street Journal*, April 12, 1972.

11. The American economy has grown and prospered over the years through a system of free enterprise more vigorous and successful than any other economic system in the world. Capital investment has produced millions of jobs and thousands of business opportunities for Americans. The success of that investment system is convincingly demonstrated in every index of the magnitude and basic strength of our economy, and in comparison with the economies of other nations.

Today our economy is faced with serious challenges. An unprecedented supply of new capital will be required over the next few years to help restore and broaden a sound, expansionary capital base through business and Government investment. In order to ensure that our capital markets continue to function fairly and efficiently to meet these challenges, it is vital that we constantly seek ways to improve their operations. Among other things, we must be sure that laws and regulations written 30 or 40 years ago do not unfairly interfere with the need for changes in our modern-day markets. It is with this important goal in mind that I am very pleased to have signed into law the Securities Acts Amendments of 1975.

THE IMPORTANCE OF COMPETITION

This act will provide important new directives to the industry and its regulators to ensure that competition is always a prime consideration in establishing or abolishing market rules. And it will continue to strengthen the rules calling for high standards of financial capability and ethical behavior on the part of those individuals and institutions that perform important market functions. (In this regard, I understand that the legislation contains an inadvertent technical error concerning the presence of a transfer agent as a jurisdictional basis for State or local taxation of securities transactions. I also understand that legislation to correct this error retroactively is being prepared and that such legislation will receive prompt consideration in Congress. When such corrective legislation is presented to me, I intend to sign it.) The act seeks to ensure that market participants function with the highest degree of efficiency and that the capital markets will themselves be orderly and accessible. The key to reaching this objective will be a new national market system for securities. The act charges the industry and the Securities and Exchange Commission to work operatively, but in the words of the House-Senate conferees, it is intended that "the national market system evolve through the interplay of competitive forces, as unnecessary regulatory restrictions are removed." No Government formula nor any industry system of exclusionary rules can match the incentives and rewards for innovation and improved efficiency, which natural competition provides.

This legislation encourages greater use of available improvements in electronic and communications technology as the basis for a fully integrated trading system. A system in which buyers and sellers are aware of the full range of securities prices will help ensure that artificial restrictions on competition no longer distort the market's true expression of supply and demand. It will also help reduce the cost of transacting trades.

The act also directs members and supervisors of securities exchanges to examine rules that tend to limit the number and variety of participants eligible for membership. Open competition within exchanges is just as important as competition among different markets. The right to enter these markets and provide a necessary public service should not be subject to arbitrary institutional rules, which limit competition. It is my hope also that the SEC will, in the process of helping to shape the national market system, take steps to eliminate obsolete or overlapping regulations, which unnecessarily constrain the market.

I also want to stress the importance of the SEC's decision to disallow all fixed rates of brokerage commission previously set by those firms and individuals which comprise the securities industry.

It is my strong belief that government has unwisely condoned a wide range of anti-competitive price regulation. My Administration will continue to press for legislative reforms to amend or abolish such practices. I commend the SEC for its efforts, and the industry for its cooperation, in reaching the important goal of freely competitive pricing for a full range of brokerage and other services. I am confident that, in the long run, this policy will produce a much healthier industry.

NEW PROTECTIONS FOR INVESTORS

Public confidence is a vital ingredient if our capital markets are to continue to attract a wide variety of investors. Though large institutions have become increasingly active as owners and traders of securities, individuals still represent the backbone of the American capital system. This act provides important new safeguards that will help insure public trust in the securities markets. Among these safeguards are new rules for brokers' financial strength and accountability. The act imposes new restrictions on "self-dealing" to eliminate a potential conflict of interest and deny institutions a special advantage over individual investors. The act further requires periodic disclosure by institutional investors of their holdings and transactions in securities.

CONCLUSION

My Administration is seeking major reforms in many Federal regulatory agencies to eliminate unnecessary restrictions and promote more efficient and competitive industries.

This legislation is the product of 10 years of intensive work by several administrations, the Congress, the Securities and Exchange Commission, and the many elements of the securities industry.

The product is a good one, and it represents the first of what I hope will be a long series of much-needed regulatory reforms.

Note: As enacted, the bill (S. 249), approved June 4, 1975, is Public Law 94-29 (89 Stat. 97).

Citation: John T. Woolley and Gerhard Peters, The American Presidency Project [online]. Santa Barbara, CA. Available from World Wide Web: http://www.presidency. ucsb.edu/ws/?pid=4970.

12. SEC Commissioner Philip A. Loomis, Jr., "The Securities Amendments of 1975, Self–Regulation and the National Market System," Joint Securities Conference Sponsored by the NASD, Boston Stock Exchange, and the SEC, Boston, MA. Nov. 18, 1975.

12

Precursor

It came with the suddenness and surprise of a rogue lightning strike. At 11:40 a.m. on Monday, October 19, 1987, a cascade of selling overwhelmed the stock exchanges and specialists, taking the Dow Jones Industrial Average (DJIA) by the end of the day down by 508 points. This arguably was the largest one-day decline since the Great Depression, and the losses were catastrophic. Investors were $1 trillion poorer when the closing bell sounded than they had been when the trading had ended the previous Friday. An 800-point rise in the DJIA during the previous ten months was trimmed by 63.5%.

The market had been falling the previous two weeks as institutions engaged in panic selling (see Figure 12.1). But Wall Street analysts remained bullish. When the DJIA staged a 37-point rally on Columbus Day following a 159-point drop the previous week, Kidder, Peabody & Co. confidently had advised clients that a long-term bull market remained intact.[1]

Other investment experts had been equally as rosy. Robert Prechter, who the *Wall Street Journal* described as the reigning market guru, predicted in the first *Barron's* cover story of 1987 that the DJIA would hit 3,600. Prechter, editor of the *Elliot Wave Theorist* newsletter, seemed prescient. The DJIA rose to what was to be its high that year of 2,722.42 in August—a level that contrarians felt was overvalued.[2]

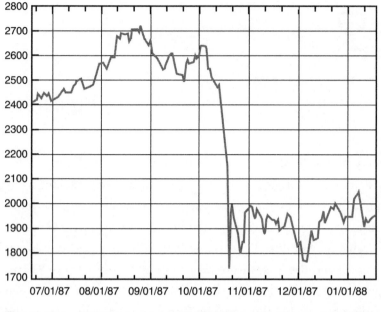

Figure 12.1   Dow Jones (June 19, 1987 Through January 19, 1988).

Source: Wikipedia

But this had been a year of buying frenzy fueled by takeovers funded by junk bonds. The deals enriched corporate raiders, investment bankers, and investors, and the fever had not abated even when one of the era's most successful buccaneers, Ivan Boesky, had been taken down on fraud charges by a young U.S. attorney named Rudolph Giuliani.

Analysts cited the takeover boom plus a surge in cash from foreign and American investors as the basis for their bullish predictions.[3] The public was so eager to swallow their malarkey that the market had continued its climb even when interest rates suddenly turned upward in April. The bulls ignored subsequent interest rate increases in August and September as well.[4]

There had been at least one disturbing augury: In 1986, John Phelan, chairman of the New York Stock Exchange (NYSE), had warned that an explosion in "program trading" could cause a market "meltdown."[5]

"What Phelan foresaw was that the combination of portfolio insurance and index arbitrage could create a chain reaction. By selling heavily in the futures pits, the computer guided, portfolio insurance firms would create a gap between the cache and futures markets that in turn would trigger index arbitrage in the form of purchases in the pits and sales on the floor. The arbitrage sales on the floor would drive down the underlying price to the point where the computers would call for the next round of portfolio insurance sales in the pits, and the process would repeat itself until neither the futures contracts nor the stocks had any market value at all," wrote author Martin Mayer in December 1987.[6]

Phelan's dire prediction had little effect on investors, who likely thought him a proper Luddite. In any event, the bull market of 1987 seemed to have proven him wrong.

Throughout 1987, stock brokers were so comfortable with predictions of the market's upward trajectory that they were putting Ma and Pa and the wheelchair-bound grandma next door into *naked puts*, a terribly risky market bet that can wipe out the purchaser of such a contract if the market falls.

When you invest in a put, you essentially agree for a price to insure someone else's stock against decline. You are the seller of the put. The counterparty pays you a premium, permitting her to *put* stock to you at an agreed-upon price before the put expires, which can be in months or days, depending on when you sell it. Every put has an expiration date.

Let's say that a certain stock is trading at $40 per share and you are convinced it is going to $45. You can sell a put allowing someone to sell the stock to you at $38 in the next three months should it fall $2. If you do not own the underlying stock, you are said to be *naked*. What this means is that if the stock goes to $30 or even $0, the investor has a right to make you buy her shares at $38. You may sell your contract beforehand in such a case, but you will take a loss, because the price you receive for someone to take it off your hands likely will be much lower than the premium you collected when the stock was rising.

Hundreds of brokers sold naked puts to ill-informed investors, assuming the bullish market gurus really could predict the future. One broker spoke after the crash of having talked about 70 clients into adopting the strategy, advising them that it was only moderately risky, "barring a nuclear attack or a crash like 1929."[7]

On Black Monday, 1987, these "naked" investors lost hundreds of thousands of dollars that they didn't have. Many of them were forced to declare bankruptcy. A single customer of Charles Schwab Corporation with inadequate funds to cover his losses cost the firm $15 million. In Texas, a 56-year-old quadriplegic woman lost all her savings—$35,000. In Alexandria, Virginia, a retired civil servant who had delved into naked puts lost the $54,000 in his brokerage account plus an additional $318,000. A retired engineer in Niagara Falls, New York lost $500,000, most of which had been set aside in trust for his grandkids.[8]

A presidential task force appointed by Ronald Reagan and nicknamed "The Brady Commission" by the press because it was chaired by Treasury Secretary Nicolas Brady, looked into the 1987 crash and found causes that, in retrospect, were eerily similar to the causes of the 2010 Flash Crash. Within 9 weeks, the Brady Commission performed a remarkable autopsy of the complicated chain of events responsible for the Black Monday 1987 crash and made recommendations to Congress that would have helped to prevent the 2010 event had they been followed. But the recommended reforms were never enacted because the Reagan administration, the Congress, and the regulators all had vested interests in maintaining the inadequate status quo.

Then, as now, the markets were not artfully integrated. Separate rules for the separate exchanges resulted in disconnects between the cash market, the equity market, the futures market, and the stock index future market. As in the 2010 Flash Crash, on Black Monday 1987 there were cases in which one exchange would try to slow trading in the face of a cascade of selling while other exchanges did not, so that the selling pressure washed from one market to another.

The Brady Commission's primary recommendation was that the Congress create an uber-regulator at the Federal Reserve to coordinate the efforts of the Securities and Exchange Commission (SEC) and the Commodities Futures Trading Commission (CFTC).

"Analysis of the October market break demonstrates that one agency must have the authority to coordinate a few critical inter-market issues cutting across market segments and affecting the entire financial system; to monitor activities of all market segments; and to mediate concerns across marketplaces. The specific issues which have an impact across marketplaces and throughout the financial system include: clearing and credit mechanisms; margin requirements; circuit breaker mechanisms, such as price limits and trading halts; and information systems for monitoring activities across marketplaces. The single agency required to coordinate cross-marketplace issues must have broad and deep expertise in the interaction of the stock, stock option, and stock index futures marketplaces, as well as in all financial markets, domestic and global. It must have broad expertise in the financial system as a whole," it said.[9] Both the SEC and the CFTC, however, were unwilling to surrender turf to the Federal Reserve Board, no matter how much sense it made. And Wall Street was not eager to invite a new regulator to meddle in its affairs because it had the SEC fairly well trained. As for President Reagan, he had no appetite for this particular fight. This would be the last year of his presidency, and he was preoccupied with other matters. His number-one concern was bringing the Cold War with the Soviet Union to an end. At the same time, the Navy was in a shooting war with Iraq, and his administration was overseeing the cleanup of the savings and loan industry collapse.

The bottom line was that neither Wall Street nor the regulators realized how frail the market system was. Only 3% of existing shares were traded on October 19, 1987, but it was still too great a load for the exchanges and the specialists to bear.

Like the Flash Crash, the selling on Wall Street in October 1987 was triggered by a confluence of negative economic news and exacerbated by the type of runaway program selling predicted by Phelan.

Prechter shook up his followers by suddenly turning "short-term" bearish in early October. Congress suddenly introduced legislation to curb the merger mania that had been the source of so much speculation. The merchandise trade deficit was growing. And on Sunday, October 18, members of the Reagan administration had talked down the dollar during appearances on the morning talk shows.

On Monday, October 6, the first trading day after Prechter's negative statement, the DJIA fell 91.55—its largest one-day point decline to date. Market pros said the decline had been aggravated by program trading tied to a hedging strategy used by large institutions known as *portfolio insurance*.[10]

According to the Brady Commission, portfolio insurance used computer-based models to determine optimal stock-cash ratios at various market price levels. Rather than buying and selling stocks as the market moved, most portfolio insurers adjusted the stock-cash ratio within their clients' investment portfolios by trading index futures.[11]

The October 6 selloff coupled with Phelan's warning of the previous year should have gotten the SEC up on its toes. But because the decline had been fairly orderly, the agency's antennae did not rise.

Ten days later, October 16, trading volume was unusually heavy, and the DJIA fell 108 points, a one-day record. Here had been a hike in the prime rate by New York's Chemical Bank and comments by Treasury Secretary Jim Baker suggesting the administration would embrace a weak dollar policy. Investors worried that Baker's remarks would drive away the foreign money that had helped lift stocks.[12]

Between Wednesday, October 14 and Friday, October 16, the DJIA had lost a total of 250 points. Big institutional investors began to panic. According to the Brady report, $60 billion to $90 billion of equity assets was under portfolio insurance at the time of the market break. "Two consequences were evident. First, portfolio insurers were very active sellers during the Wednesday to Friday period. In the futures market, where they concentrated their activity during this week, they sold the equivalent in stocks of approximately $530 million on Wednesday, $965 million on Thursday, and $2.1 billion on Friday. Second, they approached Monday with a huge amount of selling already dictated by their models. With the market already down 10 percent, their models dictated that, at a minimum, $12 billion (20 percent of $60 billion) of equities should already have been sold. Less than $4 billion had in fact been sold."[13]

Small investors panicked, too. On Saturday, October 17 and Sunday, October 18 retail customers jammed the phone lines at mutual fund companies with sell orders. (This was the era before the World Wide Web. The SEC didn't approve delivery of mutual fund prospectuses to customers via the Internet until 2008.) Fidelity, the largest mutual fund company at the time, received 80,000 calls.[14]

On Monday, October 19 when the opening bell sounded at the NYSE at 9:30 a.m., sellers submitted $500 million in orders. By 10 a.m., the number of sells had mushroomed to $975 million. Exacerbating the selloff, was a relaxation of SEC Rule 10-A the previous December.[15] The rule prohibited selling by a brokerage house except on an uptick. The SEC, in an effort to appease the brokerage community, had decided to allow short sales into a declining market as long as one of the firm's proprietary accounts was long the stocks and the sale was pursuant to the unwinding of an index arbitrage.

Buying and selling on the floor of the NYSE largely was manual in 1987—handled by specialists required to purchase shares in their own accounts when there were no other buyers. The specialists kept an order book listing buy orders on one side and sell orders on the other. They received a commission for matching buyer and seller, which was anywhere from an eighth to a sixteenth of a dollar, depending on the stock price. They made a handsome living in this business. But on Black Monday, nearly 200 NYSE listed stocks did not open because the specialists could not match the sell orders with buy orders quickly enough. There were too many sells. They, of course, were expected to buy and sell against the trend. Although many NYSE specialists did this part of their job well, even to the point of exhausting their firms' capital (which required them consequently to merge with stronger firms), a number did not live up to their formal obligation. Some sold more stock than they bought, adding momentum to the crash. Some specialists who had bought shares on the way down inflated stock prices at the opening of October 20 to try to make sizable profits on the inventory they had purchased during the panic. The NYSE launched 15 separate investigations of specialist firms following the crash. Three firms were banned from the business. The scandal caused people to wonder aloud if machines could not be programmed to do the same jobs the specialists were doing rather poorly, and for less cost.

But truth be told, the machines didn't perform so well that day either. The NYSE had a rudimentary automated system called Designated Order Turnaround (DOT) for trading orders of up to 2,099 shares. Orders sent electronically over the system from brokerage firms to the floor of the NYSE were printed on machine-readable cards and then taken by a clerk to a specialist who in turn executed the order. When the trade was executed, the specialists marked the card and returned it to the clerk, who in turn put it into a reader that transmitted the order-confirmation back to the brokerage firm. There were 128 printers on the exchange floor. On a normal day, each one could handle up to 12 messages per minute. On October 19, the system was flooded with so many sell orders that it took up to 75 minutes to execute an order. Because of that substantial delay, a seller submitting a market order received a price much lower than the one that had been posted on the exchange's consolidated tape an hour or so earlier.

Investors were treated more shabbily in the NASDAQ over-the-counter market. The market makers there, known as *dealers*, had no obligation to stay active in the face of a rout. Some formally withdrew from market making that day. Other market makers simply refused to answer their phones. This left retail traders who were desperately trying to liquidate their positions or trying to buy stocks on the way down high and dry.

One of the victims of that day's trading on the NASDAQ was Harvey Ira Houtkin, a squat, woolly haired arbitrageur. He had a long memory and a penchant for revenge. NASDAQ would rue the day it crossed Houtkin.

Endnotes

1. Mathew Rees, "The Hunt for Black October," *The American, The Journal of the American Enterprise Institute*, September 10, 2007.

2. James B. Stewart and Daniel Hertzberg, "The Crash of '87," *The Wall Street Journal*, December 11, 1987.

3. Ibid.

4. Ibid.

5. Martin Mayer, "Some Watchdog! How the SEC Helped Set the Stage for Black Monday," *Barron's Magazine*, December 28, 1987.

6. Ibid.

7. Scott McMurray and Jeff Bailey, "The Black Hole: How Some Investors Lost All Their Money in the Market Crash," *The Wall Street Journal*, December 2, 1987.

8. Ibid.

9. Introduction to "The Report of the Presidential Task Force on Market Mechanisms" (January 2008): vi.

10. Beatrice Garcia, "Abreast of the Market," *The Wall Street Journal*, October 7, 1987.

11. Report of the Presidential Task Force, 17.

12. Mathew Rees, "The Hunt for Black October," *The American, The Journal of the American Enterprise Institute*, September 10, 2007.

13. Report of the Presidential Task Force, 29.

14. Rees, "The Hunt for Black October."

15. Martin Mayer, "Some Watchdog! How the SEC Helped Set the Stage for Black Monday," *Barron's Magazine*, December 28, 1987.

13

Birth of High-Frequency Trading

In the weeks following Black Monday, a large customer of Houtkin's seven-year-old brokerage firm, Domestic Arbitrage Group, which made markets in 500 NASDAQ stocks, lost a lot more money than he was worth. In fact, the customer lost more money than Houtkin's entire firm was worth. The losses from that one trader were so huge that Houtkin had to shutter the doors to all six of his firm's offices, which was a bitter experience for him because NASDAQ regulators had eased capital rules to help bigger, better-connected firms survive the crash but let small firms like his fail.[1]

Smart and highly aggressive, Houtkin sought not sympathy but sweet revenge. He was a resilient man with an in-depth knowledge of Wall Street and a creative streak that was relatively rare in that sunless canyon. He knew how to scrap because he had been brought up in a poor household. He grew up in a low-income housing project in the Sheepshead Bay section of Brooklyn. His father was a craftsman who made artificial limbs.[2]

Encouraged by his parents to seek a better life than theirs, he matriculated at City College of New York, planning to become a dentist. In 1967, however, his eyes suddenly were opened to a new possibility. Strapped for cash, he had talked himself into an afternoon job as an assistant to a Wall Street speculator. After working there a short time, he decided that his future lay on Wall Street, not in a dentist's office scraping teeth. He switched his major to business, and after earning his undergraduate degree, he continued on toward an MBA.

Beginning in 1973, Houtkin worked for a succession of firms. This was a brutal period on Wall Street because of the bear market that had its roots in the 1969 crash. He looked on the period as an extension of his education. About the middle of the decade, he worked for corporate raiders Carl Ichan and Asher Edelman and was inspired to start his own company, which he did in 1979.

Houtkin possessed enough experience and ample smarts to know that the market makers for OTC stocks in the NASDAQ system were cheats. They'd often display quotes at a favorable price and then, when a trader placed an order with them over the telephone—which was the preferred way they did business in those days—they'd announce that the price had changed.

Since 1984, NASDAQ had had in place an electronic trading system so that it could guarantee small investors who sent their orders through registered brokers instantaneous executions up to 500 shares. The Small Order Execution System, or SOES, made it more difficult for market makers to pull a bait and switch the way they could over the telephone. SOES seldom was used, however, primarily because not many customers knew of its existence. Following Black Monday, the National Association of Securities Dealers (NASD), reacting to shrill complaints from customers who had been unable to execute as the market plunged, passed rules obligating the market makers to offer firm quotes. Under the new regime, if the order came through SOES, the market maker was obliged to honor the displayed quote up to 1,000 shares, even if the price had moved.[3]

A light bulb went off over Houtkin's head. The trader, who wore a neatly trimmed brown beard and aviator-style lenses, perceived the opportunity to profit from NASDAQ market makers who were slow to update their SOES quotes as prices changed. He began using SOES at his brother-in-law's brokerage company to front-run the slowest, least organized market makers. Houtkin made hundreds of thousands of dollars for himself because most market makers were trying to track the progress of dozens of stocks at once, and they devoted most their attention to big institutional block trades, which were the source of most of their commissions. The market makers often were slow to update the prices of lower volume stocks. Many of them relied on older SOES terminals that did not update prices as quickly as the newer models. Houtkin learned who the worst market makers were through trial and error and legally front-ran them, owing to his faster machine. In short, some of the market makers who were cheating investors over the phone now were being nipped legally by Houtkin because they had grown sloppy and inefficient.[4]

It wasn't long before Houtkin, a short man who always thought big, launched his own day-trading firm. He conducted business more as a man on a mission than an entrepreneur. He was a day-trading proselytizer. One journalist who interviewed him said that Houtkin would talk about day-trading as long as the listener was interested and would continue prattling on even when the listener had heard enough. He trained retail investors to day-trade using SOES, charging them a training fee, and he wrote a bestseller on the subject. A master salesman, he boasted that his graduates made $250,000 to $300,000 annually by day-trading stocks. His ads touted, "Most of my clients have enjoyed success virtually unheard of in the trading community."[5] According to court papers, he himself earned more than $200,000 between March and August of 1988 after subtracting $100,000 in commissions.[6]

Over-the-counter (OTC) dealers hated Houtkin because he was eating into their profits. They derogatorily called him and his customers "SOES Bandits" and attempted unsuccessfully to have the Securities and Exchange Commission (SEC) ban him from using SOES.

Houtkin's boasts that he was teaching average Janes and Johns to make easy money earned him the enmity of state and federal regulators and members of Congress. In July 2001, NASD Regulation fined his day-trading firm, All-Tech, Montvale, New Jersey, $380,000 for misleading advertising and regulatory violations. A month later, an NASD arbitration panel awarded $456,719 to six customers in San Diego who said they were lured into his day-trading firm by deceptive advertisements and had heavy losses because they were leveraged by illegal margin loans. Houtkin's reputation had taken hits before. In 1998, court documents revealed that Houtkin had lost $392,000 day-trading in his own account while making millions in commissions and fees from his customers. The biggest blow to his empire came in 1999 when a day-trading customer who had lost $500,000, largely at another day-trading firm, went berserk and shot and killed 12 people in All-Tech's Atlanta office. A few months later, Houtkin was still touting day-trading, albeit in slightly less flamboyant language. He told a reporter in Tulsa, Oklahoma, that day-trading would not enrich everyone who tried it. But at least, he said, they should have the opportunity to try to get rich. Big Wall Street firms were trying to keep the small investor down, he complained.

Sounding like Huey Long, Houtkin stated, "We are stepping on the toes of the people who are considered elite. I have a roomful of people—in Podunk, in Tulsa, in central America—competing with the big boys on Wall Street, in Chicago, and [in] San Francisco." The big boys, he said, were saying to him and his SOES bandits, "This is my game. Get out!"

Houtkin growled, "It's not their game."[7]

NASD, which was a captive regulator, hounded Houtkin for years, looking for any infraction of trading rules on his part. At one point, the NASD banned him from the industry for six months. He seethed later to an interviewer, "That suspension was the incubation period for my total contempt for these people."[8]

He again determined that he would have his revenge. No one messed with Houtkin.

Besides SOES, OTC brokers had another electronic system called Order Confirmation Transaction, or OCT. A trader's broker would send a computer message to a market maker on OCT offering to make a trade. Unlike SOES, this system was voluntary as far as the market maker was concerned. The market maker did not have to honor the displayed price. Whenever Houtkin used the system, the market makers would either ignore his orders completely or artificially widen the spread between the bid and asked price, a violation of SEC rules. Houtkin filed close to 200 complaints against market makers for "backing away." Nothing happened.

Houtkin complained to the press and eventually became a source for the *Los Angeles Times,* which wrote an investigative series on the OCT controversy whose findings supported his claims. This engendered a Justice Department investigation. Then in 1994, Houtkin received some unsuspected help from a pair of professors, Paul Schultz of Ohio State and William Christie of Vanderbilt University, who wrote a statistical study of the entire NASDAQ market and concluded that the prices were rigged. In 1996, the Justice Department formally accused major OTC dealers of having rigged prices for years by maintaining spreads at a quarter rather than a quarter or an eighth as in other markets and using telephone pressure tactics to keep fellow traders in line with that convention. Attorney General Janet Reno said that the market makers had manipulated millions of dollars from consumer pockets. The Justice Department required all NASDAQ member firms to monitor the phone conversations by traders on their OTC desks to ascertain that they were not engaged in price fixing or other illegal activities.

The vocal Houtkin, who in October 2008 would die at age 58 after tonsil surgery, had ignited a revolution.

As a result of the scandal, the SEC decided to make changes in the market to ensure that retain investors would obtain the best prices when they bought or sold stock. In 1998, some of the larger trading electronic trading venues known as Automatic Trading Systems (ATSs), where market makers and select institutional customers had traded blocks of stock with one another at prices better than those available on the NASDAQ market, were ordered to open their doors to retail investors and publicly report their prices.

Wall Streeters had thought that the existing market structure was splendid for business. From their vantage at the top of the food chain, the New York Stock Exchange (NYSE) and NASDAQ were perfectly good retail markets, and the ATSs were perfectly good wholesale markets, where institutional investors could trade large orders with one another without distorting prices. But SEC Chairman Levitt didn't like what he saw, especially in light of the NASDAQ market maker price-fixing scandal. In his mind, it was a two-tiered market that gave institutional investors too great a pricing advantage.

"Arthur got a bee in his bonnet that somehow this was wrong. He's a bit of a populist," a long-time Wall Street executive recounted.[9] Levitt decided to let everybody buy wholesale. From now on, an investor's orders would be routed to the trading venue with the best price. It was a far-reaching decision—some legal scholars would later argue that it was an example of the type of regulatory over-reach that Moss had desired to avoid. The market would be changed in ways unanticipated by Levitt, and not necessarily for the better.

NASDAQ agreed to post all the prices of the dealers and the affected ATSs, such as the popular Instinet ATS, on its public display. This, the SEC predicted, would break the backs of the dealers because now they would have had to compete for volume with the ATS universe by pricing their stocks more aggressively. What the new regime did was anger the institutional investors, especially mutual funds. There was a new breed of trader prowling the stock market: the hedge fund. They liked to front-run institutional orders, which is why the institutions primarily had been trading in the old upstairs market, out of sight. Now the institutions would be defenseless prey for the hedge funds, which had an algorithmic advantage. The hedge funds had begun using pattern-recognition software, which could spot heavy buying and selling of specific securities and predict with an accuracy ranging from 60% to 80% how far the specific stock would move up or down on the next several trades. Thus, the hedge funds had the ability to front-run the market. They'd buy stock on an exchange where the targeted stock was priced low and go to Instinet or another ATS and sell the stock at the higher price predicted by the algorithm, knowing that big mutual funds were buying the stock in those venues.

It didn't take long for fund managers to start complaining to executives at the NYSE and NASDAQ that, because of Levitt's meddling, the marketplace had become a zoo. When they entered a buy or sell order on Instinet, they were constantly being "picked off" at the wrong price, which meant they paid too much for too little. All the rules that Levitt had adopted in hopes of improving the lot of the retail investor were working against the institutional traders. And in the end, the retail customer was hurt, too. Retail customers were the biggest purchasers of mutual funds.

The SEC rule championed by Levitt, Regulation ATS, had a big loophole in it and did not close the upstairs market altogether. The loophole required an ATS to open itself to retail investors if it breached a certain volume threshold. The threshold was liberal. An entrepreneur could make a good living catering to mutual funds if he started an ATS and kept it small so that it never breached the threshold. Thus was born the dark pool, a place where fund managers could execute at least a portion of their trades out of the reach of the hedge funds and their quantitative traders. Dan Mathisson, a Credit Suisse managing partner, would write in a June 2008 column in *Traders Magazine*, "The SEC's original release explaining the regulation said that ATSs have an 'obligation to provide investors a fair opportunity to participate in their systems,' and a series of 'fair-access' rules were defined. But the fair-access rules in Regulation ATS were poorly conceived and could be more accurately named the 'no-access' rules. The rules stated that ATSs only have to open to the public in any individual stocks where they have exceeded five percent of the volume for four of the past six months. On top of that very high bar, there was a long list of exemptions, including inexplicably exempting any ATS that systematically prices at the midpoint. And even if an ATS were to hit the five-percent bar in a particular stock, in the real world there was no way for a trader to connect to get rightful access."

Mathisson pointed out that there was no Web site or database maintained by the regulators that listed which dark pools were opened to the public in a given month. As far as was known, he said, no ATS has ever exceeded the threshold. But, then again, how would anyone be able to tell? And if a trader did somehow sniff out that a given ATS was open to the public, he'd still have to negotiate and sign contracts, run dedicated lines, and set up a system for booking and clearing trades.

"By the time you were ready to trade, the fair-access period for the stock would have long expired," Mathisson wrote.

Most ATSs would successfully stay below the 5% threshold. This in turn meant that there was not enough capacity in the dark pool universe for all of the institutional shares wanting to trade on these venues. Obviously, this was a golden opportunity to make a fortune. Traders began starting up dark pool ATSs. The market that Levitt had attempted to unify began to spin apart.

There was more fragmentation to come. In addition to dark pools, electronic communication networks (ECNs) such as ARCA and Island popped up specifically to cater to SOES bandits. NAS-DAQ itself finally built an electronic trading network called Super Montage to compete with all the new electronic venues. Otherwise, the new competitors would have eaten NASDAQ alive.[10]

As fragmentation increased, volume left the exchanges, and market makers lost business and barely could survive. The punishment meted out by Levitt had been, for many of them, a death sentence. And this had an unintended consequence that eventually would prove devastating to the economy and cost it hundreds of thousands of jobs.

The robust NASDAQ market for initial public offerings began to shrivel. A 2010 paper by David Weild and Edward Kim of Grant Thornton said that Levitt's market meddling directly had contributed to the destruction of the market for initial public offerings of new, innovative companies. During the 1990s, NASDAQ had been the primary incubator for innovative high-tech start-ups. The fledgling companies had employed hundreds of thousands of persons and had given the United States economy a substantial boost. Tax revenues from the booming sector had helped President Bill Clinton balance the budget. But, as result of Levitt's reforms, spreads for NASDAQ market makers quickly declined by more than 30%. The market makers gradually were replaced by high-frequency traders—an iteration of Houtkin's SOES bandits. From 1997 to year-end 2009, publicly listed companies traded on stock exchanges declined by 40%. At the same time, there was a geometric increase in the activities of high-frequency trading (HFT) firms. Weild did not view this as happenstance. In June 2010 testimony before the Joint CFTC-SEC Advisory Committee on Emerging Regulatory Issues, Weild accused high-frequency traders of creating "new forms of systemic risk, a loss of investor confidence, and a disastrous decline in primary (IPO) capital formation and the number of publicly listed companies in the United States."

An economic crisis was in the making, Weild indicated. "Today's market structure has lost the ability to support small capitalization companies and initial public offerings on a scale necessary to drive the U.S. economy. The U.S. now annually delists twice as many companies as it lists, and this trend has been going on ever since the advent of electronic trading," he said.

Steve Wunch, who created one of the earliest electronic stock exchanges, said Levitt's explicit desire was to bring down the market makers because he believed they were caught red-handed with their hands in the cookie jar. And the market makers were the heart of the NASDAQ system at that time. The rule change forced NASDAQ to modify its old business model and, in doing so, destroyed many of its former functions.

"The main thing we are missing today is capital formation. That's what NASDAQ did. And beginning in 1997 with the order handling rule, it stopped doing that, and no one replaced it. The great companies and high-tech advantages we created in the 1980s and 1990s are dead and gone," said Wunch.

As a result, the United States lost millions of jobs. Weild and Lee began lobbying for creation of a separate market for IPOs with wider spreads and larger commissions to bring back sales support to the stocks offered by brokers and specialists. In other words, it would be a market unaffected by Levitt's "improvements."

In 2000, Levitt's SEC landed another huge blow on the chins of the market makers and specialists, demanding that all exchanges start pricing stocks in decimals by April 2001. That meant that the spreads they had charged would be squeezed from the old high of 12.5 cents to as low as a penny per share on the most heavily traded stock issues. It pushed many hangers on out of business. But the change was a bonanza for investors, big and small. By 2002, retail traders were reporting a 50% reduction in their transactions costs.

Specialists at the NYSE remained a thorn in the side of many traders. The 1975 "Trade-Through Rule" remained in effect. The rule that required an exchange to send a customer's order to a competing exchange if the competing exchange was posting had a better bid or asked price. The specialists at the NYSE and at the American Stock Exchange (AMEX) often posted better prices, especially for exchange-traded funds (ETFs), which were growing in popularity. But the posted price that the investor saw on the consolidated tape was not the price that the investor received. The specialists had 30 seconds in which to respond to an order, and often the price would move up or down during that brief interval.

For electronic traders, 30 seconds was an eternity. Some of them were trying to implement complex hedging strategies, and the timing of the hedges was of paramount importance to them. Consequently, these traders were willing to execute their orders quickly at a fully electronic exchange, even if it meant paying a slightly higher price than the best one displayed at the NYSE or the AMEX.

Island, an ECN that was a spinoff of Daytek, a day-trading firm, began catering to the computer traders by ignoring the trade-through rule. Island argued that it had a fiduciary duty to provide its customers with the "best execution" and that at times best execution meant fastest execution, not lowest-priced execution. The SEC appreciated the distinction and offered Island a compromise: It would allow Island to "trade through" the AMEX and the NYSE if it was offering its customers a price within three percentage points of those competing exchanges. Island viewed this as a step in the right direction. Still, it did not think the SEC had gone far enough. The trade-through rule, in essence, provided an unfair competitive advantage to the old exchanges, it argued. So Island declared that rather than comply with such an anticompetitive rule, it would become a dark pool. Island subsequently went dark, losing half of its volume in the process.

Former SEC Commissioner Paul Atkins said, "Island's refusal to enter the national market system due to the anticompetitive nature of the trade-through rule produced a firestorm of debate within the industry and created a policy dilemma for the SEC. The ECNs argued that the trade-through rule was anticompetitive and protected manual exchange volume. The exchanges argued that the trade-through rule offered important investor protection against executions at inferior prices. Finally, some investors wanted the freedom to determine how and where to execute their own transactions."[11]

Island's revolt caused the SEC to reconsider the trade-through rule and to press ahead with the adoption of Regulation NMS in 2005, one of the worst examples of regulatory arrogance in history. The heavy handed, "we-know-best" approach taken by the SEC as it crafted Regulation NMS would distort the stock market so that it would become unsafe for long-term investors and a play land for high-frequency traders.

It was SEC Commissioner William H. Donaldson, a former Wall Street executive, who finally gave the go-ahead to proceed—a full 30 years after Congress had instructed the SEC to establish a national market system. The SEC staff convinced Donaldson that computer technology had reached a level to allow it to design a workable, fully integrated system of exchanges. But as Ohio State Law professor

Dale Oesterle pointed out in a provocative 2005 paper, the SEC exceeded Congress's original mandate in crafting the regulation. Congress, Oesterle wrote, never intended the SEC to micro-manage the behavior of the participants in a national market system. Yet that's what it had been doing from the reign of Levitt on forward.

SEC Commissioners Cynthia Glassman and Paul Atkins voted against adoption of the regulation and then took the highly unusual step of publishing a 44-page dissent. The pair of protesting regulators wrote that the regulation was detrimental to competition and innovation and that many of its policy changes were arbitrary. They presciently warned that the SEC had constructed a market edifice that was so complicated that unintended consequences would be the result. But they were Republicans. Levitt and the other commissioners were Democrats who believed that their Republican colleagues were playing politics, so they ignored their protest.

Regulation NMS forced all the alternative trading venues such as Island and Instinet to register as either an exchange or a broker. It adopted a new trade-through rule for the electronic age that said you could not trade through the lowest displayed quote at an exchange if the exchange responded within 1 second.

"Strangely, the NYSE supported this," said a former SEC official who was there at the time. "This was really a bad move on its part."

The reason was that the NYSE had to become an electronic exchange itself to respond in 1 second. Shortly after Regulation NMS became effective, its share of the volume in NYSE-listed stocks fell from 80% to 25%.

This volume decline, in turn, helped set the stage for the Flash Crash. One reason is that no one but the SEC had the authority to halt all trading in a particular stock. And it was impractical for a variety of reasons to expect the SEC to exercise this power. The main reason, of course, was that the SEC wasn't equipped to monitor daily trading activity.

When the NYSE had 80% of the volume, the market halts were not an issue. If the NYSE declared a halt in trading in a particular stock, trading halted everywhere. The other exchanges would have been crushed by buy or sell orders if they did not follow suit. But when the NYSE's share dropped to 25%, none of the other exchanges followed its lead anymore. However, the SEC didn't catch on to this. The regulatory agency was proud of the big changes it was engineering in the market and it viewed the results through rose-colored glasses.

So because of this regulatory hubris, this commissar-style meddling in the free marketplace, when trading became chaotic on May 6, nobody had a clue as to how to stop it.

Endnotes

1. Gretchen Morgenson, "Outsider Trading: Regulatory Heat Is Nothing New for Harvey Houtkin, The Day Trading Guru," *National Post*, Ontario, Canada (August 20, 1999): C 9.

2. Ibid.

3. Jerry W. Markham, *A Financial History of the United States, Volume III* (Armonk, New York: M.E. Sharpe, 2002): 185.

4. Thomas G. Donlan, "Terrors of the Tube: Computerized Traders vs. Market Makers," *Barron's Magazine* (November 7, 1988): 13.

5. Gregory Bresinger, "NASD Hammers Controversial Day Trader," *Traders Magazine*, July 1, 2001.

6. Ibid.

7. Shaun Schafer, "Day Trade Advocate Defends Democracy," *Tulsa World*, October 14, 1999.

8. Morgenson, "Outsider Trading."

9. Author interview in July 2010.

10. Author interview with Robert Colby.

11. Paul S. Atkins, SEC Commissioner, "Speech Before the Boston Securities Traders Association," March 9, 2005.

14

Evil Geniuses?

There was nothing particularly flashy about high-frequency traders. A typical proprietary shop consisted of computer jocks, some math and physics wonks, and a handful of old-fashioned traders, many who had cut their teeth either in the push and shove and throat-scraping roar of the commodities and options trading pits in Chicago or on the proprietary trading desks of big New York banks.

One thing that high-frequency traders had in common was a preference for the covert life. They preferred life in the shadows as opposed to life in the limelight because they guarded their trading secrets as carefully as anglers protect their favorite fishing holes. Now, in the wake of the Flash Crash, a publicity spotlight had been aimed at their habitat, and accusing fingers were waved in their faces, so they decided to fight back as best they could. They believed that their prosecutors were badly misinformed and that their industry was being subjected to hanging justice. The mob consisted of jealous competitors such as Arnuk and Saluzzi, who were seeking a regulatory advantage to protect their bread and butter from the more efficient and technologically superior high-frequency traders. Lots of accusations had been leveled at them, but no one had pointed to a single line of code in a high-frequency algorithm that showed they were manipulating the markets. The Securities and Exchange Commission (SEC) had altered the market's rules in 1997 and again in 2005, and the high-frequency traders simply had been visionary in their exploitation of those changes. Now they were under attack for their inventiveness. It was like the horse-and-buggy trade trying to get Model T cars banned from Main Street because the new technology spooked their horses.

Progress always posed a threat to some corner of the economy. During the nineteenth century in Great Britain, textile artisans known as the Luddites attempted to protect their manual, home-based spinning industry by burning factories that used mechanized looms to produce bolts of cloth in greater volume and at a much lower cost. The same dynamic of creative destruction was at work on Wall Street, where computers proved they could trade faster and smarter than humans.

Most of the high-frequency traders hoped the controversy would blow over so they could concentrate exclusively on making money. And there was considerable money to be made. One high-frequency trader revealed that his proprietary trading firm made an annual return of 300% merely buying and selling stocks in short time frames over the course of each day. The high-frequency trading (HFT) firm made a profit virtually every day of the year. The exception was on days when the firm introduced an untested trading algorithm to exploit some newly discovered pricing inefficiency in the market. Then unanticipated glitches often popped up and cost the firm money until the formula was fine-tuned. But that was just a small cost of doing business.

Although high-frequency traders felt they occupied the high moral ground, it wasn't an adequate defense. A few high-frequency traders were familiar enough with Washington, DC, to appreciate the threat it posed to their firms. The heavy hand of government rested on the controls of the securities and commodities market system. Consequently, companies and special interests regularly tried to manipulate the Congress and the regulators to eke out competitive advantages for themselves. Traditional market players had long relationships with the regulators and Congress. For HFT firms to remain politically inactive was to invite the opposition to pull on some political strings and cut off their legs at the knees. So in the summer of

2010, a well-financed public relations effort was launched in cooperation with the Futures Industry Association of America, the influential commodities market trade group. During that time, some HFT owners stepped up and became industry apologists on their own.

Richard Gorelick of RGM in Austin, Texas, was one of the high-frequency traders who chose to shed his anonymity and rise to the defense of the HFT industry. Bright and personable, he was an excellent choice for an ambassador. He enjoyed meeting people and liked spending time in the limelight. He happily appeared in Washington, DC, on behalf of the industry at several events hosted by the SEC and by the Commodities Futures Trading Commission (CFTC).

The good-natured Gorelick described himself as a "recovering lawyer." During the 1990s, he migrated from a big New York legal firm to an Internet start-up, Deja.com, a shopping comparison site where he served as a corporate counsel. He transitioned into a business role, and he liked it. The technology bubble burst in 2000 before Deja.com could bring an initial public offering (IPO) to market. It sold its shopping service to EBay and its newsgroup search archive to Google.[1] Gorelick spent the next six months consulting and mulling over different career options. During that hiatus, he had some discussions with a former colleague—Robbie Robinette, who had a background in physics—about using sophisticated computers to trade stocks. Mark Melton, a software developer who specialized in machine learning and was Robinette's cycling partner, soon joined the discussions. None of them had a trading background. They didn't feel they needed that experience. They had been speculating that if people could make money drawing lines on stock charts and yelling at each other across trading floors, they could do the same with a more scientific approach. They foresaw opportunities to expand as the market became more computer driven. So in 2001, Robinette, Gorelick, and Melton launched RGM, running it from Robinette's living room in Austin, Texas. Their first foray into the market earned them $17 in profits. They had been running a program they had written to arbitrage statistical relationships among stocks.[2] A year later, they were renting office space and hiring employees.

The trio was visionary because this was four years before the adoption of Regulation NMS, which would create more arbitrage opportunities for high-frequency traders by inadvertently spawning new exchanges and trading venues and fragmenting the market. By 2010, RGM could boast on its Web site of employing "one hundred professionals, including software developers, information technologists, and scientists with backgrounds in computer science, physics, chemistry, statistics, and ecology."

Manoj Narang was another high-frequency trader who stepped forward to defend the besieged industry. From a barebones office above the Restoration Hardware store at 54 Broad Street in Red Bank, New Jersey, a seashore-area town on the banks of the Navesink River, he waged a gloves-off, one-man public relations effort to debunk critics like Saluzzi and Arnuk, whom he characterized as being either ignorant or deliberately deceptive.

Narang did not think the markets were perfect. Far from it, he believed regulators had made them needlessly complex. But he bristled at those who blamed all the markets' problems, from volatility to the Flash Crash, on high-frequency traders.

In Narang's mind, panicky long-term investors stampeding for the market's exit, all at the same time, triggered the Flash Crash. They similarly had triggered crashes in the past and would do so in the future. It was a fact of life in the markets. High-frequency traders, in his view, had prevented the Flash Crash from becoming a genuinely catastrophic event. The markets had bounced back on May 6 because high-frequency traders had started buying, he argued.

Narang was dark, slim, and handsome and spoke in a rich baritone. His hair and goatee were jet black, with traces of silver. He was friendly, patient, and forceful, and he had a gift for lecture. He had hung a white board in his office to illustrate his arguments.

After graduating from MIT in 1991 with a degree in mathematics and computer science, Narang began working on the proprietary trading desk at First Boston, engaging in statistical arbitrage. He expected the job to be temporary. His plan was to return to academia in a year or so to obtain a Ph.D. in mathematics, but he was bitten by the Wall Street bug. Narang discovered that he enjoyed trading, so he traded virtually everything, from Treasury bonds to equities. Over the next eight years, he worked for a number of Wall Street's largest firms, including Goldman Sachs. While at Goldman Sachs, he decided to launch his own business. He had spied a niche in the market that no one was serving—one that he thought offered potential for profit and for providing a public service. So in 1999, at the apex of the tech bubble, Narang secured funding from some investment bankers and launched a company called Tradeworx at Park Avenue and 27th Street in Manhattan to provide sophisticated, algorithmic decision-making tools to the retail clients of online brokers.

The online brokerage industry was fairly new at the time, yet it had managed to radically transform the brokerage business, capturing 40% of all retail market equity orders in a span of about a year and a half.

"I thought that it was incredibly exciting on the one hand and incredibly dangerous on the other because all these people had new-found access to the markets, newfound access to information," Narang recalled. "It was a big leveling of the playing field. But it wasn't clear to me that people had the training to deal with all that information. The premise behind Tradeworx was to create a suite of investment decision support tools that could help people at every stage of the process, from investment selection [and] idea generation to two-portfolio design, to trade execution, to you name it," he said.[3] He saw his role as democratizing the use of advanced technology in the market by bringing it to retail investors.

Narang's business model was along the lines of Google's: There was complicated machinery behind the scenes driving these tools. But

all this was hidden from the user, who saw nothing but a simple inter-
face on his computer screen, like icons to double-click.

The most popular tool enabled investors to calculate the best limit
price for buying and selling a specific stock. He used the example of a
businessman who wanted to place an order for IBM before heading
out to a meeting for an hour or so. The businessman did not want to
buy the stock at the current offer price. He wanted to bargain—to
submit a lower bid. But he also wanted at least an 80% chance of having the order filled by the time he returned to the office. In the past,
he simply would have pulled a number out of the air. Retail investors
did this all the time, but it was terribly inefficient. The average
investor had no idea if the stock would be inclined to rise or fall from
its current posted price. He had no idea how to compute the probability of his bid being taken within a certain time frame. But this was a
fairly straightforward proposition for a well-designed computer algorithm. So the Tradeworx tool would tell the businessman exactly the
price that would give him the best odds of getting his bid hit within
the required time frame. It removed the guesswork out of a common
investment decision—whether to use a market order or a limit order.

The tools were posted on the home pages of sites like CNBC.com
and AOLfinance.com. Leading online brokerage firms paid Tradeworx 10 cents anytime one of their clients clicked on one of the tools.
The limit-order calculator was used more than 20 million times in its
first six months on the Internet.

Tradeworx had dozens of similarly unique and innovative tools.
The SEC purchased some of them for its Web site for a few years,
including a margin-risk calculator that would compute the odds of a
portfolio receiving a margin call and recommending specific trades to
reduce the odds by 10% to 20%.

As was the case with most dot-com startups, Tradeworx's
expenses outstripped its revenues in the early years. When the 9/11
attacks occurred and the capital markets shut down, Tradeworx could
not find additional sources of venture capital. Narang decided that he

had to use the company's technology to make money in the market to keep the young company afloat. So Tradeworx became a hedge fund and, later, established an HFT business.

Gorelick, Narang, and other apologists for the HFT industry argued that their trading improved all the markets, particularly the equities market. Retail investors who once had been gouged by over-reaching by Wall Street specialists—those middlemen at the exchanges who maintained artificially wide spreads between the bid and asked price of a security—were now enjoying the lowest transaction costs in market history. Spreads of the most frequently traded stocks were merely a penny! Commissions were at all-time lows. And customer orders were now executed in seconds, so there was less fear of the market moving away from the posted price between the time a customer submitted an order and the time the order found a buyer or a seller. HFT spokesmen also waved academic studies they had commissioned "proving" that high-frequency traders were reducing market volatility by bringing new liquidity to the exchanges and not, in fact, adding to the volatility, as critics charged.

As for the Flash Crash, Narang argued that the SEC had created a market system that was overly complex and simply would exacerbate the problem if it drafted a host of new regulations aimed at curbing the activities of high-frequency traders. It was better to remove some of the regulations adopted in 1997 and 2005 than to pile on new ones and make the market even more complex, because complexity increased the chances of another crash.

Gorelick viewed the attack on his industry as venting by cranks and crackpots. Any crank who had been harboring a gripe about, say, market structure decided that this particular pet peeve had been the root cause of the Flash Crash. Some of the cranks blamed pretrade risk controls at the exchanges for the crash. Some of them blamed a cutthroat algorithm gone wild. Others said that HFT in general was a problem. With the Flash Crash as a backdrop, said Gorelick, each of the cranks turned his particular gripe into a griping, dramatic story.

High-frequency traders conceded that there might be some bad apples among them. Bad apples, they argued, were to be found in virtually any industry. But, this being said, high-frequency traders insisted that the accusations regarding market manipulation were unfounded.

A major part of the image problem for the HFT industry was that few people on Wall Street or in Washington, DC, understood exactly what high-frequency traders did that was of measurable value to the markets and to the economy. High-frequency traders were not transparent, and they were unregulated. No one could say exactly how many HFT firms existed or how much money they pocketed. All that was known about them was that beginning in 2007, HFT shops began multiplying faster than rabbits in the outback of Australia.

Industry data was unreliable. In 2009, high-frequency firms supposedly represented just 2% or about 400 of the estimated 20,000 trading firms in the United States, but they accounted for 73% of all U.S. equity volume. The Tabb Group, a consulting firm catering to HFT firms, estimated that their combined annual profit was about $21 billion.[4] A year later, Tabb Group estimated that roughly 150 of the HFT firms traded U.S. equities and that their gross trading profits would total $5.6 billion.

Narang argued that HFT generated $2 billion to $3 billion of trading revenue per year in U.S. equities. He told the High Frequency Trading Review in June 2010 that if one multiplied the penny-per-share profit margin of a typical high-frequency trade by the amount of daily HFT volume, which he estimated at 10 billion shares, the sum would be $2 billion in annual profits.

Narang complained, "Some firms, like TABB, have grossly overstated the amount of HFT revenues by expanding the definition to include algorithmic trading in general, regardless of the actual holding period of the trader. Large stat-arb firms,[5] which hold positions for multiple days, are not engaging in HFT. By definition, if you are able to hold positions for that long, you are not part of the HFT arms race, and [you] don't need superfast technology to access opportunities before they disappear!"

Narang had a narrow definition of HFT.

Some high-frequency traders were large firms such as Getco and Tradebot Systems, both of which were market-making firms that provided the same services once delivered by specialists. Getco registered as a New York Stock Exchange (NYSE) specialist firm, and its competitors believed it was trying to convince regulators to make all HFT firms engaged in market-making activities to register with the SEC and adhere to strict capital standards, a change that would have driven many of the smaller trading firms out of business. Banks and Wall Street brokerages also established proprietary high-speed trading desks. But the majority of high-frequency traders were smaller proprietary trading shops or "prop shops," which had no outside customers. They clustered around New York and Chicago to be close on the one hand to securities markets and on the other to the Chicago Mercantile Exchange (CME).

The public often mislabeled high-frequency traders as "Quants." The term is short for quantitative traders and refers to graduates of elite schools such as MIT and the University of Chicago whose inventiveness over the past 30 years has brought marvelous wonders to the marketplace. These wonders include options and derivatives, credit default swaps, and mortgage-backed securities—advanced tools for an advanced economy—that were badly overused and ended exploding the aforesaid advanced economy in 2007.

Quants rely on scientific principles as opposed to discretionary judgments when making investment decisions.[6] Richard Bookstaber, a college professor turned Quant turned SEC regulator, described Quants as "people who can build financial products and trading models by combining brainiac-level mathematics with massive computing power."[7]

However, the public was off only by a little bit: High-frequency traders constituted a separate branch of the same evolutionary tree.

They traded at much faster speeds and had much shorter attention spans than the Quants, but they employed some of the same arbitrage techniques. But for high-frequency traders, speed is the most important edge in their arsenal.

Many of these Wall Street physicists had been trained by universities funded in part by Defense Advanced Research Projects Agency (DARPA), which was formed in 1958 in reaction to Sputnik to rejuvenate the nation's defense technologies. In short, it was created to wreck havoc on the Soviets, not deliver a black eye to capitalism. Critics of these traders viewed them not only as a blight on Wall Street, but also as a terrible waste of government resources. They should have been at work in science labs, Ken Safian, of Safian Research, complained. And the Quants and the high-frequency traders were misusing discoveries that had been made on behalf of the national security establishment, other critics asserted. The sort of algorithms that the Quants employed to trade on multiple exchanges across markets, for example, had been pioneered by government laboratories seeking ways to track the telephone and e-mail traffic across multiple continents. Likewise, it was the advances in parallel computing at these government labs that led to the development of the type of lightning-fast servers that the high-frequency crowd used. IBM, working at Los Alamos National Laboratory in New Mexico, built the government a supercomputer known as Road Runner that can process a quadrillion calculations every second. The machinery occupies 6,000 square feet of space.

High-frequency traders by 2010 were using nitrogen-cooling systems to overclock their machines. Overclocking enabled computer processors to run much faster than they were designed to run, so they could run more operations and digest more data. In this way, HFT firms could do millions of complex trades a day. Even faster equipment was forecast for the years ahead with computers driven by photons rather than electrons, which in theory would reduce the time it takes to transmit data to optical interfaces such as monitors.[8]

"It's become a technological arms race, and what separates winners and losers is how fast they can move," said Joseph M. Mecane of NYSE Euronext in July 2009.[9]

Quants built the first complex models to predict the movement of interest rates and equities, and they wrote algorithms to buy and sell the specific securities required to keep their portfolios properly adjusted to take advantage of the expected market moves. These later were adopted by the HFT firms and adapted for shorter trades. Quants also were experts in statistical probability and would analyze historical data for patterns thought to repeat under certain circumstances, believing that future uncertainty could be reduced by collecting such information. For example, certain buzz words in the minutes of a Federal Reserve Board meeting might affect the stock market in a specific way. High-frequency traders eagerly embraced this kind of pattern-recognition software.

The Quants, who predated the HFT industry by 20 years, often founded hedge funds as opposed to trading exclusively on their own dime. This practice invited regulatory scrutiny and the associated expenses whenever a member of the Quant fraternity had an exceptional meltdown. The SEC tried to regulate hedge funds in the wake of the Long Term Capital Management (LTCM) hedge fund debacle in 1998, but the courts threw out its rules. Congress eventually stepped in and required regulation for some of the larger hedge funds in the Dodd-Frank Financial reform Law of 2010. So a spotlight had been shone on that industry.

Quants in the late 1990s and early 2000s learned the hard way what should have been fairly obvious—the longer one's time horizon, the more difficult it is to predict the future. Any meteorologist or political prognosticator could have told them that. It was this eureka moment that ushered in the era of what is now known as HFT.

Previously, the Quants had chosen investments with durations of months or even years. LTCM had Nobel Prize laureates Myron Scholes and Robert C. Merton on its team. The hedge fund made a highly leveraged, long-term bet on the direction of interest rates. That bet went haywire about a year after it was made when Russia unexpectedly defaulted on its sovereign bonds. They might have done better of they had called the fund Short-Term Capital Management.

Likewise, dozens of hedge funds swallowed huge losses when the mortgage markets blew up in 2007. They had made long-term bets that housing values, which had risen almost every year since the end of World War II, would continue to go up and up, beyond the financial stratosphere.

How could people who are remarkably intelligent behave so recklessly? Because the strategies worked long enough to make them rich. It's hard to argue with success. According to MIT professor Andrew W. Lo, "Although a national decline in home prices was certainly possible, historical experience suggested [it] was highly improbable. Therefore, it is not surprising that during the period from 1998 to 2006, senior managers of major financial institutions were not concerned with this risk—the last such event was too far back for anyone to care about, especially given how much financial markets have changed in the interim."[10]

Also, the quantitative players had unrealistic faith in the predictive power of their algorithms. The formulas were limited by the imaginations of their creators, who saw no such limitations in themselves. Because of this, the algorithms might react to certain unanticipated market conditions in ways their creators never envisioned.

The Quants may not have paid close enough attention to recent history. During the Cold War, the Russians were "algorithm addicts"; they relied on algorithms heavily for their nuclear command and early warning systems. On September 26, 1983, a false alarm of a U.S. missile launch sent to a nuclear command center by a Russian satellite was caused by an algorithm that had not been calibrated to deal with certain unanticipated conditions, said Bruce Blair, president of the World Security Institute. It was the most dangerous false alarm of the Cold War.[11]

From 2007 on, short-term trading became the new rage. Some high-frequency traders thought in a time horizon spanning a few seconds at most, and they never held a position overnight, because that was too risky. News of an earthquake or a terrorist attack in some part of the world could cause assets to lose value by the time the market opened the next day. It was better, then, for the risk-adverse, high-frequency trader to end the trading day flat, with no positions on the books.

In general, high-frequency traders favored four strategies.[12] The most publicized strategy—the one least offensive to the public and the politicians—was *automated liquidity provision*, in which high-frequency traders functioned like market makers, making millions of trades each day to earn sub-penny rebates per share from exchanges for bringing volume to those venues. Another strategy, called "sniping" and which brought the traders considerable public relations problems, tried to identify large orders in the market by using algorithms to detect trading patterns in small orders that showed they were flowing at intervals from a single source, such as a pension fund or a mutual fund. Credit Suisse, a large provider of HFT solutions, hawked algorithms to traders with names like "Guerilla" and "Sniper" to detect big orders in both the public markets and in dark pools, where mutual funds, pensions, and other big buyers and sellers attempt to trade without rippling the markets. A third strategy, called *event trading*, tried to capitalize on the news of the day and predict which direction the markets would take in reaction to the latest development. Harvey Houtkin used to instruct his trading students, "The trend is your friend," and this was a variation of that theme. Large quantitative-trading firms such as Medallion engaged heavily in this type of momentum trading. The fourth strategy was old-fashioned *arbitrage*, in which the traders attempted to find price discrepancies between seemingly unrelated instruments, like stocks and sugar futures, for instance. Generally speaking, the algorithms compared data of past stock and commodities movements to build an understanding of how they might behave in the present. This allowed computers programmed with these algorithms to look for pricing inefficiencies. If on a given day a stock rose in value by X dollars, for instance, the traders might judge the move to be extreme, based on 20 years' worth of pricing, volume, and related data, and short the stock, expecting it to correct back down. If the underlying company was a big food producer, the stock's fall might affect the prices of agricultural futures on the commodities exchange. The super-fast computers would exploit such correlations.

Statistical arbitrage was a variation on the age-old theme of buy low and sell high, but with some twists. For instance, a trader did not always buy and sell exactly the same stock. The trader could buy a high-tech stock such as Microsoft when it was trending lower and immediately sell an index or exchange-traded fund (ETF) of high-tech stocks such as the QQQ, which has Microsoft as a component and would adjust downward to reflect Microsoft's lower market value.

This strategy revolved around the notion of a fair price. HFT firms designed algorithms to determine the fair price of a particular stock at a given time by looking at dozens of correlations. Typically, stocks oscillated around their fair price. The traders plotted the price points over a period of time and then smoothed the data to create a mean value. If a stock was trading above that mean, the algorithm assumed it was overpriced and a candidate for a short sale. If the stock was below the mean, the algorithm would judge it to be undervalued and buy it. A high-frequency trader would short dozens of overpriced stocks and buy dozens of underpriced stocks and close the positions as the prices converged, all in a matter of minutes.

High-frequency traders considered most fundamental investors to be sloppy. Take the case of an institutional investor who unloads a large block of Apple, a transaction likely to drive down the price. The institutional investor is pleased with this particular transaction because he's made a long-term capital gain. In the view of the quantitative trader, however, the institutional investor has lost more money than he made because he neglected to short all the future indexes and

ETFs that have Apple as a component. He's also neglected to short related stocks and to place buy orders below the market on the ones likely to pop back up when the trade is digested by the market. Average traders are looking at the market as though it only had one dimension. High-frequency traders think of average traders as members of the flat-earth society, headed for certain extinction because they can't figure out all the angles. Average traders, they contend, should let machines make all their decisions. In fact, many big funds use computers for much of their trading.

The machines bought and the machines sold, and they didn't care what they were selling as long as they could get rid of the shares in 2 minutes or less. The machines were dominating the market. What did all of it mean?

Jeff Silver and Ben Hunt, managing directors of Iridian Asset Management, tried to answer this question in a letter to their investors at the end of the second quarter of 2010. "At its most basic level, it means that the prices of securities bear little or no relationship to the fundamental economic reality of the corporations that issue those securities," they wrote. "It means that price discovery, which is the fundamental goal of the open bid-ask system of a public exchange, is no longer meaningful on terms that make sense to the investor whose decisions are based on fundamental economic reality. It means the U.S. equity market is no longer an effective capital market where shares of a stock represent ownership interest in an economic entity with cash flows and assets, but is more accurately conceptualized as a casino where shares or stocks are simply placeholders for money—chips."

The high-frequency trader was playing the markets the way card counters play blackjack, they said, providing liquidity if a market for a particular security is staked in his favor and backing off at other times.

One would have thought the stock exchanges would have raised an alarm. But they were so hungry for cash they gave the high-frequency traders the equivalent of a stacked deck in return for their patronage, arguing with them that it was all for the benefit of the public. And how did the grateful public react? They fled.

Endnotes

1. Kambiz Forohar, "Trading Pennies into $7 Billion Drives High-Frequency Cowboys," Bloomberg.com, October 6, 2010.

2. Ibid.

3. Interview with the author, September 28, 2010.

4. Rob Iati, "The Real Story of Trading Software Espionage," *Advanced Trading* magazine, July 10, 2009.

5. Stat-arb firms use statistics to predict the direction of stocks and then invest in other assets, like commodities, that tend to move in relation to those stocks. This exploitation of related securities is called arbitrage.

6. Irene Aldridge, *High-Frequency Trading: A Practical Guide to Algorithmic Strategies and Trading Systems* (Hoboken, New Jersey: John Wiley & Sons, Inc., 2010), Kindle Edition, Location 514–521.

7. Richard Bookstaber, *A Demon of Our Own Design: Markets, Hedge Funds, and the Perils of Financial Innovation* (Hoboken, New Jersey: John Wiley & Sons, Inc., 2007), Kindle Edition, Location 154.

8. "Discovery Brings New Type of Fast Computer Closer to Reality," ScienceDaily.com, September 28, 2009.

9. Charles Duhigg, "Traders Find That Speed Pays, in Milliseconds," *The New York Times*, July 23, 2009.

10. Andrew W. Lo and Mark T. Muller, "Warning: Physics Envy May Be Hazardous to Your Wealth!," MIT Sloan School of Management, March 19, 2010.

11. E-mail from Bruce Blair to the author, August 3, 2010.

12. Aldridge, Location 188–196.

15

Dirty Rotten Scoundrels

Now that the NASDAQ and New York Stock Exchange (NYSE) were publicly traded companies, they had to answer to stockholders, who naturally wanted a handsome return on their investment. It was a far cry from the days when the NASDAQ and NYSE were member-owned duopolies that functioned more or less like public utilities. The two, large exchanges were forced to scrape for trading volume against several dozen rivals ranging from automated exchanges to dark pools to 200 internalizers—those brokerage houses that matched trades in house. It wasn't long before the exchanges woke up to the fact that high-frequency trading (HFT) firms were a flock of golden geese. Their trading translated into huge amounts of share volume. This, in turn, increased an exchange's share of revenue from the sale of trading data placed on the consolidated tape, the high-speed, electronic system that constantly reports the latest price and volume data on sales of exchange-listed stocks.

The Consolidated Tape Association collected and posted the data on the Consolidated Tape System and sold it to brokerage houses, hedge funds, news organizations, and other end users. At the end of every year, the association apportioned the net revenues from those sales. The exchanges that had generated the greatest trading volume received the largest slices of that revenue pie. The total amount of the Tape Association's revenues was a closely guarded secret. In 2002—the last time that the association's financials were released to the general public—the Consolidated Tape Association reported gross revenues of

$424 million and net income of $383 million. Market volume had exploded since then, and gross revenues in 2010 were estimated to be several billion dollars.

Some of the exchanges began paying high-frequency traders for executing trades on their venues. The traders received a small rebate each time they bought a stock or, in the parlance of the industry, each time they brought *liquidity* to the exchange. The rebates were a fraction of a penny for each share. NASDAQ OMX in October 2010 paid its highest-volume high-frequency trading customers .00295 per share. Lower volume traders received less. A number of trading firms' computers would trade the same thousand or so shares of a stock such as Citigroup back and forth between each other all day long just to earn those rebates, which added up to real money at day's end. Citigroup set a U.S. record for the most shares traded in a single day on February 27, 2009, when 1.87 billion shares traded hands—most likely because of high-frequency trading.

Critics such as Arnuk and Saluzzi compared this practice to a game of extended volley between two tennis players. If the players hit the same tennis ball a million times, back and forth across the net all day long, did an observer count a million balls or merely one ball? The exchanges were adding up the thousand shares in the order each time the trade occurred and using the sum to denote the total volume. Arnuk and Saluzzi said this was sham accounting—the volume wasn't real, and it gave the false impression that the markets were more liquid than they actually were.

Speed, of course, had become the ultimate competitive edge in the new electronic marketplace. It was right out of the world of computer gaming, where a slight speed advantage can give one's animated character or *avatar* a quicker draw than the other hombre. In an onscreen animated gun battle, the avatar that moves the slowest ends up getting blown away. Now the same dynamic was at work in the stock market: The buyers or sellers who were not as speedy or nimble as the HFT firms were "picked off." The high-frequency traders could see their orders coming into the market before anyone else could and consequently could front-run them. They'd buy up the shares the slow investor wanted and then turn around in a fraction of a second and sell the stocks to that slow investor for a penny-per-share profit, and sometimes more. High-frequency traders could buy a stock and turn around and sell it in a split second. They seldom held on to a position for more than two minutes. They were not fundamental investors. They didn't care what a company's earnings might be for the next quarter or for the next week or even for the next 10 minutes. HFT firms were aiming for a surefire profit, even if it was measured in fractions of a penny for each share. Holding a stock more than 2 minutes was risky because the markets were so unpredictable.

Appreciating the appeal of speed, exchanges began to invite brokerage firms, especially those with HFT desks, to connect their trading machines directly to the exchange's own servers, a practice known as *collocation*. The hookups were costly but well worth it to these firms. Algorithms ran the HFT machines. The machines in effect were making thousands of buy and sell decisions on their own every second; and by being hooked into the exchange machines, they could buy and sell more stock even faster because *latency*, the time it took for electrons to travel from point A to point B, had been physically shortened.

"If you're in Greenwich, Connecticut, and you place an order to buy a stock, it could take a half-a-thousandth of a second for the order to reach an exchange. But if your computer is sitting in the same building with the exchange's matching engines, the computers that put buyers and sellers together, your order gets to the exchange 50 times faster," said Vasant Dhar, a former high-frequency trader who ended up teaching trading strategies at New York University's Stern School of Business.[1]

Demand for collocation was growing so rapidly, owing to the rise of automated trading, that huge facilities began to spring up around trading centers like Chicago and Manhattan. Equinix, a trading firm, built a colocation facility the size of five football fields four miles west of Manhattan in Secaucus, New Jersey.[2] The NYSE Euronext built a facility for its matching engines the size of seven football fields in Mahwah, New Jersey, and invited HFT firms to collocate there.

Mahwah is an Indian name that translates to "where paths cross." Exchange officials made a big show of planting six buttonwood trees outside the warehouse-like facility to reference the NYSE's Wall Street roots, where trading supposedly began under a buttonwood tree at the tail end of the eighteenth century. The shade of the buttonwood tree was free. The NYSE Euronext expected its Mahwah operation to become a $1 billion business.[3]

The brokers, in turn, saw a way to profit by subletting space on their servers at these collocation facilities. They began to offer "naked sponsored access" to their HFT constituents, including hedge funds. This meant that the brokers had vouched to the exchanges that the high-frequency traders who were subletting server space from them were upstanding, adequately capitalized citizens who could be trusted to settle their trades and not to deliberately manipulate the markets or employ an algorithm that might suddenly issue crazy buy and sell orders and disrupt the markets. However, critics thought it was preposterous for the exchanges to believe that the brokerage houses had actually vetted the HFT firms, which by nature were super-secretive. The critics said the arrangements posed a number of serious threats to the overall market. An HFT firm, for example, might go broke and yet continue to trade before anyone realized it, hoping to make itself whole again. This scenario was not farfetched. In 2003, a U.S. trading firm became insolvent in 16 seconds when an employee who had no previous involvement with algorithms switched one on. It took the company 47 minutes to realize it had gone bust and to call its clearing bank, to apprise it of the situation.[4]

Most HFT firms were collocating machines at multiple exchanges in both the equities and commodities markets, and the exchanges always welcomed these customers with open arms. Regulation National Market System (NMS), which had fostered competition among the exchanges to reduce costs to investors, had created a market in which HFT firms could thrive and so change the nature of trading that it became toxic for most everyone else.

Endnotes

1. Jill Barshay, "High-Speed Trading Goes Off the Street," *Market Watch*, August 26, 2009. http://marketplace.publicradio.org/display/web/2009/08/26/pm-colocation/.

2. Ibid.

3. Jacob Bunge, "DJ NYSE Euronext Turns on NJ Data Center as Emigration Begins," Dow Jones News Wires, August 25, 2010.

4. Carol L. Clark, "Controlling Risk in a Lightning-Speed Trading Environment," Chicago Fed Letter, March 2010, No. 272.

16 ———————————————————————————

Dark Pools

High-frequency trading (HFT) apologists insisted that their activities, net-net, had made the stock market a far better place for investors than it had been in the past. If that was the case, wondered the Commodities Futures Trading Commission's (CFTC's) Andrei Kirilenko at a hearing in August 2010—if the HFTs were not in fact the voracious sharks that critics made them out to be—why were all the other fish behaving so strangely? Why did mutual funds and pension funds feel the need to hide from algorithmic traders in dark pools, those trading venues where their orders were invisible to the market at large?

Dark pools had proliferated after the Securities and Exchange Commission (SEC) under Levitt tried to dismantle the wholesale market in 1997 to force the block trades of pensions, mutual funds, and other institutional traders onto the exchanges. The dark pools were markets in which the institutions could come to conduct block trades, as long as the volume of those trades remained under a certain threshold. It was as if the government had set a limit on the amount of food a grocery store could sell. If that ever happened, thousands of smaller groceries would spring up to satisfy public demand. This in effect is what happened in regard to dark pools. Dozens sprang up to meet demand because none wanted to exceed the government's 5% threshold. (See Chapter 13, "Birth of High-Frequency Trading.")

If you were trading in a dark pool, which was an over-the-counter (OTC) market, you did not have to post your buy and sell orders on the consolidated tape. The orders were invisible and did not affect pricing in the broad market. The institutions could choose to post the sale price of the stock to the tape after the fact, but there was no hard-and fast requirement to reveal detailed volume information.

By 2009, dark pools had gotten under the skin of the New York Stock Exchange (NYSE) because they were draining volume away from the exchanges. NYSE Euronext CEO Duncan Niederauer complained to Senator Schumer about this. In October 2009, Schumer and Niederauer wrote a joint letter to SEC Chairman Schapiro recommending a series of reforms for dark pools because "These darkened corners of the market hurt transparency and compromise the market's fundamental function of price discovery."

The SEC subsequently asked the public for comments on a proposal to make the dark pools more transparent. It asked investors to report if price discovery on the lit exchanges had indeed suffered as a result of the growth of dark pools. The SEC also was curious to learn if investors thought the volume lost to the dark pools by the lit exchanges such as the NYSE had increased spreads and contributed to short-term volatility.

The dark pools, for their part, argued that they traded so close to the publicly posted price that their transaction did not negatively affect the broader market at all.

The SEC had noted in a January 2010 concept release on market structure, "It appears that a significant percentage of the orders of long-term investors are executed either in dark pools or at OTC market makers, while a large percentage of the trading volume in displayed trading centers is attributable to proprietary firms executing short-term trading strategies. Has there in fact been an increase in the proportion of long-term investor orders executed in undisplayed trading centers? If so, what is the reason for this tendency, and is the practice beneficial or harmful to long-term investors and to market quality?"

In other words, had the high-frequency sharks chased long-term investors into these shadowy hidey-holes?

It was obvious that this had occurred. Pipeline Trading LLC, a dark pool, had a video demonstration on its Web site that featured animated sharks attempting to attack institutional orders. Pipeline not only crossed institutional large orders, it offered institutions anti-gaming software that allowed them to slice their block of stocks into 300-share orders to avoid the sharks when they searched for buyers and sellers in the broad or "lit" market.

"We offer technology that usually is used to prey on the institutions and turn it back on the predators to prevent them from recognizing a pattern in order flow," said Alfred Berkeley, the company's chairman.

The SEC's concerns were not in line with empirical evidence according to dark pool advocates. "Today 70% of the market volume is on exchanges and 30% of the market is off exchange. That's been true for several decades. So the amount of volume on the exchanges versus off actually hasn't changed in a very long time," said one dark pool operator.

Seth Merrin, the founder and CEO of Liquidnet, a dark pool that has been operating since 1999, said his idea was to provide a wholesale market in which big institutions could trade among themselves without moving markets and without getting front-run by the speculators.

"We took our cue from every other market out there that separates its wholesale market from its retail market," he said.

Merrin's idea made him a billionaire, a fact that seemed to impress others more than it impressed him. He was soft spoken, laid back, and deferential. He was also very hands on. He had been the dark pool industry's most visible and tireless advocate. He had spent many hours in Washington, DC, making the rounds to regulators, the press, and members of Congress to argue the case for leaving the dark pools alone.

Liquidnet was registered with the SEC as a broker dealer as opposed to a stock exchange. Liquidnet's customers primarily were large institutions with average trades of 150,000 shares. Liquidnet matched "size with size" to avoid the sort of supply-demand imbalances that could roil the market.

Merrin argued that one market could not satisfy all trading constituencies:

"You would not find a buyer from Macy's going to the corner Gap to buy a million shirts; nor can you expect Fidelity to buy a million shares on the NYSE or the NASDAQ at 300 shares per shot. It does not work. You have to separate wholesale from retail."

It was a complex issue. One thing Merrin's camp had going for it was that the SEC was loathe to decide such a complex issue for fear of making the market even worse than it had become.

17 ─────────────────────────

Volatility Villains

The investors who fled the market following the Flash Crash were responding to the perception of increased intraday volatility. Since 2008, the daily market roller-coaster ride had become wilder and more unpredictable than any in memory. Moves in the stock averages that once took the better part of a year were occurring in a matter of hours. The Dow Jones Industrial Average (DJIA) might climb 50 to 100 points before noon and give it all back by 4 p.m. A company's shares could spike up or down independent of a specific news event or any change in the company's underlying fundamentals. In the 20 years prior to the Great Recession, the equities market had been far less turbulent. Now it appeared as wild and risky as the commodities market. Volatility charts of stock market activity looked like a bottle brush, with all the action between 2008 and 2010 (see Figure 17.1).

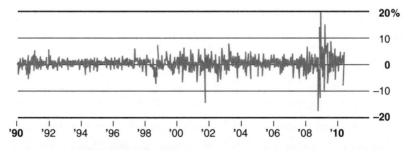

Figure 17.1   Bad case of the jitters: The stock market, as measured by the Value Line Index, has become far more volatile since the financial crisis that began in late 2008.

Reprinted from *Barron's Magazine*

The unstable environment created a perfect habitat for high-frequency traders. The more volatile the market became, the greater the opportunity for consistently fantastic, short-term gains. The high-frequency traders piled up profits, whereas slower investors lost cash and faith in the market as their stock positions were whipsawed up and down.

There was a rhythm to the volatility. Most of the trading volume occurred in the early morning and in the late afternoon, with a period of eerie quiet in between. It was as though the market had been replaced by one made in Italy, where workers for centuries had embraced the long, relaxing lunch break between their busy mornings and their busy evenings. Activity on America's stock exchanges became so quiet around the noon hour that some high-frequency traders took to taking time off during the midday to attend the cinema or to run personal errands. Kristina Peterson of *The Wall Street Journal* profiled one small firm whose three principals walked several miles from Wall Street across the Brooklyn Bridge one afternoon to dine at their favorite pizza-pie emporium. In the old days, they never would have left their trading desk for fear of missing out on a big opportunity. In the old days, a trader could not set his watch by the volatility. The change made retail investors suspicious that the HFT firms were market puppet masters and that they choreographed the volatile minuet—a charge that the HFT firms repeatedly denied.

Thomson Reuters compiled data showing that half of a typical day's market volume occurred in the opening and closing minutes of the trading day. In August 2010, nearly 58% of New York Stock Exchange's (NYSE's) primary volume took place between 9:30 a.m. and 10:30 a.m. and between 3:30 p.m. and 4 p.m. In August of 2005, those hours had seen 45% of the day's volume. The rise of high-frequency trading (HFT) amplified the concentration of trading at the beginning and end of the day, analysts said.[1] HFT firms, in some cases, exploited the daily, end-of-the-day rebalancing of leveraged exchange-traded funds. These funds' asset managers traded the stocks in their funds in near lockstep at the end of each day to keep their leverage ratios' constant. The high-frequency traders wrote algorithms that could determine if a leveraged exchange-traded fund (ETF) would be buying or selling on a particular day, allowing the HFT firms to front-run those orders. Under certain circumstances, the analysts found, leveraged ETFs could constitute 75% of the trading volume at the market close.[2]

Not everybody blamed HFT firms for the volatility. One popular theory held that the general behavior of investors had become over-correlated. Essentially, they were all doing the same thing every day. If everyone on the deck of a cruise ship ran to the port rail and then over to the starboard rail and continued to run back and forth like this, the ship would sway wildly. The investors had rushed into ETFs and S&P index futures and stock options and other instruments that were based on the broad markets or on large sectors of the economy so they could take advantage of price and momentum trends. When they bought or sold these broad indexes practically at the same time, the markets made extreme moves.

Picking out a single stock for one's portfolio had become a mug's game, the equivalent of buying a lottery ticket. So, too, had long-term investing. Investors who had lost their shirts in 2007 and 2008 now held onto their investments for shorter periods. They had been badly scalded by following the conventional wisdom about stocks being the superior investment over the long term. Like sage cats, they'd never again jump on that stove top. The game now was to make 15% to 20% in a few weeks like the big boys at the hedge funds.

Investors who had been raised on the fundamentalist dogma of Benjamin Graham and David Dodd were close to despair. Stock-picking had become a dead art. Macro-themed investing was the rage. The market ignored earnings and cash flows and other life signs of the underlying securities.[3]

Some market economists continued to cite the contribution of economic and political uncertainty as the primary cause of investor skittishness. In Europe, spring and summer debt crises in Spain and

Portugal had been succeeded in the fall by one in Ireland. At home, the Federal Reserve's policy of easy money was having scant impact on economic growth. Additionally, there was an important mid-term election looming, which made investors nervous. Would there be gridlock on Capitol Hill? Would left-leaning, anti-business Democrats retain control? Would capital gains taxes on the wealthy rise? These questions hung over the market like storm clouds; and the uncertainty was unlikely to vanish after the election. There were serious trade problems with China; an alarming breakdown of law and order in Mexico; and indications that radical Islamists were gaining control of nuclear-armed Pakistan. The world was a frightening place.

"I suspect that the new patterns in the equities market that led to this volatility are so well established that it will be some time before the volatility diminishes," said Jim McCaughan, CEO of Principal Global Investors. He expected it to last as many as 5 to 10 years.[4]

High-frequency traders, sensitive to the backlash against their kind, attributed it to a combination of ignorance and professional jealousy among investors who had failed to embrace advanced trading technologies. They trotted out academic studies, some by virtual unknowns and others by professors on their payroll, which argued the HFT practitioners actually reduced market volatility through their incessant trading and arbitrage, which added volume to the market and quickly eliminated pricing inefficiencies.

The studies were badly wanting, however, because they relied on narrow data. And research on intraday trading swings was relatively new, so there was no long-term record for meaningful historical comparison.

The answer might lay in the structure of the stock market that had taken shape after the actions of the SEC under Levitt and Donaldson. Whatever the cause, the exchanges were growing worried.

NASDAQ Chief Economist Frank Hathaway stated, "Higher volatility sends investors into less risky assets, which has a negative impact on exchange volume and a negative impact on the cost of equity capital."[5]

Heightened volatility was not an entirely new market phenomenon. In fact, experts expected a flare-up after the 2007 to 2008 credit crisis and subsequent market "crash" because it had occurred in the past after other big market breaks. Heightened volatility lasted for several years following the Great Depression and Black Monday in 1987. If you looked at a chart from the 1930s to the present, you would have seen a picture that resembled a barbell as opposed to a bottle brush. Scholars said the current bout of volatility would fade away on its own as soon as economic growth resumed, returning confidence in the country's long-term outlook. In fact, the equities and bond markets during the worst days of the recent credit crisis had signaled that conditions would settle down, said G. William Schwert, the Gleason professor of finance and statistics at the University of Rochester's William E. Simon Graduate School of Business. Schwert was one of the foremost experts on market volatility and had written extensively about it for many years. The professionals, through their choice of investments, Schwert said, had telegraphed to the market that it was unlikely the country would slide into a major depression, a real concern into 2010.

As for the apparent upsurge in intraday volatility beginning in 2008, there was no way of telling if it was greater than in the past owing to the absence of a historical record. But Schwert conjectured that the intraday measures of the past would look much like the daily measures, which in turn would look much like the monthly measures. Monthly data was available and indicated that volatility in 2009 and 2010 was lower than it had been after the Great Depression, a time when there were no HFT computers.

"Days that look volatile are typically volatile intraday. Months look volatile because there are days (within them) that look volatile. As a general rule, if you crank up the microscope and look at finer and finer slices of the data, your observations don't change your sense of market volatility," said Schwert.[6] This had to be true, in his opinion. If it wasn't true, there would have to be huge reversals in the stock market every day—daily flash crashes, so to speak, where the market would spike up and spike down and finish the day nearly flat to give the impression that the day had not been volatile at all.

In 1990, Schwert had written a pioneering paper on the topic of market volatility for the *Financial Analysts Journal* that looked back at Black Monday and other market dislocations and asked many of the same questions about market volatility raised by investors after the Flash Crash. He found no evidence that computer trading had contributed to increased volatility on that dark day; nor was there evidence that the volatility had been engendered by trading in futures and options based on the Standard & Poor's (S&P) 500, products that had been introduced in 1982.

"I suspect that the current debate about intraday volatility would take on a different tenor if it could be documented that recent events are not unusual," he wrote.

Other market experts, however, did not see fit to describe the 2007 to 2008 stock market declines as a "crash." Cleveland Rueckert, an analyst with Birinyi Associates, was one of them. He felt a fairer comparison to be the market decline from 2000 to 2002. Both were orderly and not symptomatic of a sudden break. Yet from 2007 to 2009, there were more than twice as many days with 3% moves in the S&P 500 than in the prior period, including 23 in 2009, when the market was recovering. In 2010, there were eight such days as of the end of November, which was above average. Even so, Rueckert said there was not enough evidence to finger a particular source for the volatility.

A theory, advanced by former quantitative trader Yan Yaroshevsky of New Jersey, was that high-frequency traders reduce volatility at certain times and exacerbate it at other times. Yaroshevsky, who immigrated to the United States from Russia in the early 1990s, helped Senator Kaufman shape his view of the HFT menace.

"When times are good, they [HFT firms] have high participation rates in the marketplace. When volume is high, they intermediate a large number of orders because there are (profit-making) opportunities for them," Yaroshevsky said.[7] Under these circumstances, they arguably reduced volatility by narrowing spreads on stocks. At the same time, Yaroshevsky said, they increased trading costs for institutional investors through front-running and other "sniping" techniques.

The press held the perception that most HFT firms were engaged in market-making and rebate-trading strategies and held no positions overnight, he said. But Yaroshevsky, who knew the industry from the inside, said this was wrong. The greatest number of HFT firms, which in his definition included any hedge fund and quantitative trader who used low-latency technology and collocation to execute trades across markets, were using short-term momentum strategies. These strategies exacerbated market volatility by driving stocks much higher or lower than they would have moved if investors merely were weighing the underlying fundamentals of the securities.

Yaroshevsky saw things occurring in the equities market that had never occurred in the past, like the market beginning to rise robustly during a recession, as it did early in 2009. The rise was driven purely by quantitative trading, he argued. Credit was first extended by the regulators at the Federal Reserve to the bankers and "into the more capable hands of the quantitative geniuses," he chuckled. Their trading drove the market higher and culminated in the Flash Crash.

It wasn't deliberate market manipulation, in his view. So many Quants employed the same momentum strategies that the market simply became divorced from its fundamentals.

"You have all these folks doing the same stuff, and the stuff works; and the more it works then the more that they do it," Yaroshevsky said.

In Yaroshevsky's opinion, then, the retail investors who had fled the marketplace were not fleeing from an imagined monster. Stocks were trading up and down for no good reason other than that HFT computers had predicted this was the direction they should go. An investor who purchased a share in a promising company could not depend on it maintaining its correct value. Pricing had become capricious, and long-term, retail investors eschewed caprice. They had been wise to run to safer havens, even if the investment returns were low. At least the returns were steady.

Endnotes

1. Kristina Peterson, "The Traders Who Skip Most of the Day," *The Wall Street Journal*, September 10, 2010.

2. Jason Zweig, "Will Leveraged ETFs Put Cracks in Market Close?," *The Wall Street Journal*, April 18, 2009.

3. Tom Lauricella and Gregory Zuckerman, "Macro Forces in Market Confound Stock Pickers," *The Wall Street Journal*, September 27, 2010.

4. Interview with author, October 6, 2010.

5. Interview with author, August 2010.

6. Interview with author, July 2010.

7. Interview with author, September 2010.

18

The Investigation

In 1987, the Brady Commission took just nine weeks to produce its report on the causes of Black Monday, which was a considerable accomplishment. The Securities and Exchange Commission (SEC) and the Commodities Futures Trading Commission (CFTC) produced a preliminary Flash Crash report by May 18, but their final report would not be ready until late September. There were numerous reasons for the longevity of the Flash Crash investigation. The primary one was that the SEC lacked direct access to the market data needed to draw a credible conclusion. The agency had to collect the data from Financial Industry Regulatory Authority (FINRA) and from each of the exchanges. The data came in several formats, and it sometimes lacked an adequate audit trail to allow investigators to piece together a complete picture of market activity that day. SECs investigators also felt the need to acquire secondary information in the form of testimony and interviews from market participants to flesh out the story told by the tape.

The SEC picked up the pace of its information gathering within a few weeks, inviting a roundtable of experts on high-frequency trading (HFT) to its headquarters on June 2 for a public discussion of the pluses and minuses of computerized trading. Schapiro had urged Kaufman to watch her, and he was—like a hawk. He didn't like what he was seeing. A spy had leaked him a list of the panel's participants in advance, and it was laughably lopsided in favor of high-frequency traders. They were to occupy six of seven seats on the stage. The Senator could hardly believe his eyes.

Kaufman angrily wrote a protest letter to Schapiro and then took to the floor of the Senate to bring his complaint to the attention of his colleagues and the press. He said, "It appears as though it (the panel) was chosen primarily to hear testimony that reinforces the top-line defenses of the current market structure—that high-frequency trading provides liquidity and reduces spreads—rather than a deep dive into the problems that caused severe market dislocation on May 6 and damaged our market's credibility. I have called on the SEC to add more participants to give the panels some semblance of balance. Frankly, Mr. President, I find the preliminary reports to be so stacked in favor of the entrenched money that has caused the very problems we seek to address that the panel itself stands as a symbolic failure of the regulators and regulatory system—that is, with the exception of a few brave souls who have been invited to critique the conventional industry wisdom."

Five of the panelists had written letters to the SEC prior to May 6 commenting on its proposed reexamination of the National Market Structure. All of them said they were in favor of the status quo.

Kaufman said one expected panelist wrote: "Over the past 18 months—since the height of the financial crisis—the Commission has been very active with rule-making proposals. Nearly all the issues that may have contributed to diminishing investor confidence have been addressed by Commission rule-making."

Kaufman said that a second expected participant, a representative of a stock exchange, had written a widely disseminated e-mail stating that the equities market was not broken. The e-mail said, "To the contrary, we would argue that the U.S. equity markets were a shining model of reliability and healthy function during what some are calling one of the most challenging and difficult times in recent market history."

A third participant wrote the SEC in advance of the meeting, "Implementing any type of regulation that would limit the tools or the effectiveness of automation available for use by any class of investor in the name of 'fairness' would turn back the clock on the U.S. equity market and undo years of innovation and investment."

The only mutual fund company invited to sit on the panel was Vanguard Funds. It was an outlier among mutual fund firms in that it staunchly defended HFT, arguing that the activity kept costs down by narrowing stock spreads and reducing transaction costs. Vanguard had a personal agenda: It was one of the largest managers of exchange-traded funds (ETFs), a product that was a cross between a mutual fund and an index option. Arnuk quipped in a blog that Vanguard churned out ETFs faster than Hasbro churned out Hannah Montana toys. Most mutual fund companies were of the mind that high-frequency traders were actually raising their trading costs by using algorithms to front-run their orders. True, spreads had narrowed—but there was a hidden tax on the mutual fund industry and its 90 million customers as a result of this front-running, they claimed.

Around this time, an asset manager described to *The Wall Street Journal* what he learned when conducting a test to see if he was being disadvantaged by high-frequency traders. One day in March 2010, he submitted an order to his broker to purchase shares of Nordson Corp., a manufacturer of precision dispensing equipment for the application of industrial liquid and powder coatings, adhesives, and sealants.[1] He wanted the order directed to a dark pool, which is invisible to the broader market, with instructions to pay no more than $70.49 per share, the midpoint between the current bid and the current ask price. The market price stayed the same. He then sent another order to the broader or "lit" market to sell Nordson for a price that moved the midpoint to $70.47. Almost immediately, his buy order in the dark pool was taken. He ended up paying 2 cents per share more than he should have had to pay. Someone with an ultra-fast computer had been lurking in the dark pool.

To assuage Senator Kaufman, the SEC quickly issued invitations to Kevin Cronin, director of global equity trading at INVESCO, a mutual fund complex, and Professor Michael Goldstein of Babson College, who suggested instituting a speed limit for computer trades. Another professor who had been invited as an independent expert, it later turned out, had been a paid consultant for some HFT firms, which made Kaufman even angrier.

MIT professor Simon Johnson, writing about the stacked meeting for the *Huffington Post* on May 28, neatly captured Senator Kaufman's frustration: "The technical fact-gathering activities of bodies like the SEC are of critical importance in both building an overall consensus ('Do we have a problem? What should we do about it?') and creating a basis for regulatory action (for example, the SEC does not even collect the data needed to understand how May 6 contributed to the May 6 disaster). Anyone who has ever put together a relatively complicated discussion of this nature can attest that how you frame the issues is typically decisive."

The problem with the SEC was that it traditionally did not want to offend any of its constituents. Building a consensus meant to the SEC drafting a solution that would not rock anyone's boat. And so all summer long it had a series of these roundtable events, and they began to sound as if they had been scripted. The high-frequency traders, like the gang members in *West Side Story*, argued they were not bad, merely misunderstood. The critics kept claiming there were strange happenings in the market that were borderline illegal, but they could not produce a smoking gun.

In perhaps what was his most frustrating experience as a senator, Kaufman failed to get Banking Committee Chairman Senator Chris Dodd, a fellow Democrat, to add language about HFT and naked short-selling to the financial reform legislation he was crafting with Representative Barney Frank of Massachusetts, chairman of the House Financial Services Committee. The bill would be the most far-reaching overhaul of Wall Street and banking in 20 years.

Said Senator Kaufman, "We went to people and we said, 'There's this incredible problem.' Their basic thinking was, number one, it has got to be something that demonstrably was part of the problem that brought the market down, and high-frequency trading and naked short selling were not part of that problem."

After the Flash Crash, Senator Kaufman convinced Senator Mark Warner of Virginia to coauthor a letter to Dodd asking that Dodd add a provision to the financial reform bill requiring the SEC to study HFT and report its findings to the Congress. Dodd refused.

"And it wasn't because Dodd didn't care," said Kaufman. "It was just, 'We don't need this now.' We couldn't even to get the SEC to do a study—which they have to do anyway."

Perhaps Dodd was unaware of everything in his own bill. As the complex bill was hastily being cobbled together prior to its passage in July 2010, the staff of the CFTC pulled a fast one on the high-frequency trading industry. The staff members convinced Republican and Democratic members of the Senate Agricultural Committee to slip a provision in the bill allowing the regulatory agency to prohibit practices it deemed "disruptive of fair and equitable trading." "Spoofing" in the commodities market would be banned outright by the law. No one seemed to notice. The provision was buried in a section of the 2,300-page bill that deals with the trading of credit default swaps by commercial banks. Four months after the passage of the Dodd-Frank Act, the CFTC would shock the HFT industry and begin using "Section 747" of the act to draft curbs on HFT activity in the commodities markets, even as the SEC continued to twiddle its thumbs.

The HFT industry was focused on the threat from Schumer and Kaufman. Its first strategic move following the Flash Crash was to establish a lobbying front to combat the two senators. The high-frequency traders had the formidable Futures Industry Association on their side. The new lobby convinced two Republican members of the House Financial Services Committee, Spencer Bachus of Alabama, and Jeb Hensarling of Texas, both avid deregulators, to write a letter to SEC Chairman Schapiro advising her not to rush to judgment and blame May 6 on high-frequency traders. The letter was as close to cheerleading as they could come without looking like industry prostitutes. It also was a not-so-subtle warning to Schapiro to watch out, because if the GOP lived up to the expectations of pollsters, the party would take control of the House in the November 2010 midterm election, in which case Bachus would become chairman of the Financial Services Committee, with oversight of both the SEC and the CFTC.

Feeling the heat and anxious to prove that it was on the ball, the SEC in mid-June decided to run a six-month trial of a market-wide "circuit breaker" rule for the individual stocks in the Standard & Poor's (S&P) 500 to prevent future flash crashes. In September, it expanded the trial to also include all stocks in the Russell 1000 index. All exchanges were instructed to halt trading for 5 minutes in any stock whose price moves 10% or more, up or down, within 5 minutes. This was the solution favored by the high-frequency traders, and arguably it was cosmetic. But the SEC implemented it quicker than the average highway department installs a speed bump.

The fact was that the SEC did not seem to appreciate the exact nature of the disease that had infected the stock market. Experienced asset managers on Wall Street saw it. Because of HFT, the entire equity market had become a gigantic derivative product with no underlying value. This was the same phenomenon that had brought down the credit markets in 2007. The machines looked at historic price discrepancies and bought stock on that basis. The machines didn't care what the name of the underlying company was or what its future growth potential was. Machines did not discriminate on that basis. The machine merely tried to predict if a stock would go up or down over the next several minutes. And it wasn't just the machines that had lost touch with market fundamentals. Those retail investors who stayed in the market were playing the momentum game, not investing. They wanted to go with the flow, to ride the trend. Thus, they were inclined to buy stock-index futures, options, and ETFs that mimicked the S&P 500 or specific sectors of the economy. As far as the small investor was concerned, the classic buy-and-hold strategy had been a big bust. The market was a lightning-fast roller coaster, and you had to sell at the top of the hill before the market took you screaming to the bottom.

Even if an investor had wanted to buy stocks the old-fashioned way—by pouring over its financials and weighing the informed opinions of star analysts—he would have found himself at a disadvantage compared to times gone by. Credible, inexpensive analytical reports had become a rarity. Investors had to spend money to make money. They had to subscribe to a pricey service like Value Line or Market-Grader for in-depth company reports. Brokerage firms were not providing as much free analytical commentary to their clients as they once did. Few of them even maintained analytic departments anymore. Eliot Laurence Spitzer had inadvertently seen to that. In 2002, when he was riding high as New York attorney general—exposing the alleged mendacity of Wall Street analysts who never wrote a discouraging word about companies with whom their firms had lucrative investment banking relationships—Spitzer came down too hard. He demanded that all Wall Street firms agree to delink analyst pay from investment banking activities.

One analyst who came under Spitzer's fire was Henry Blodgett, who covered high-tech companies for Merrill Lynch. He had been sued in 2001 by an angry pediatrician, Debases Kanjilal, of Queens, who lost $500,000 investing in InfoSpace Inc., which creates Internet search engines. This was during the "tech wreck," when Internet start-ups began losing money hand over fist. Investors lost $4.7 trillion when the Internet bubble burst, sending the prices of highly speculative tech stocks tumbling.

Dr. Kanjilal claimed his Merrill Lynch & Co. broker had urged him not to sell when the stock was trading at $60 a share because it was a Blodgett favorite. By the time the physician stopped listening to his broker and sold his holdings, InfoSpace was trading at $11 per share. It eventually hit $3.

Kanjilal said, "I lost all my money for my children's education fund. I was devastated, I was angry, I was frustrated, and I was totally disappointed."[2]

He filed an arbitration claim against Merrill Lynch in March 2001, arguing that Blodget had misled investors by fraudulently promoting the stocks of companies with which the firm had investment banking relationships. Spitzer smelled a good case and decided to investigate. A few weeks later, he released e-mails from Blodgett in which Blodgett referred to some of the stocks he had recommended as "crap."[3]

The investment banking departments of the firms had been subsidizing the analysts, whose reports were handed out free to clients great and small. Ethically, the delinking of the investment banking departments from the analysts made sense. But from a practical standpoint, it was not the wisest course. Spitzer threw the proverbial baby out with the bathwater.

Not all analysts had been disingenuous. Some had been quite good, offering insights beyond commentary on balance sheets, ratios, and cash flows. The analysts were well versed in industry gossip, knew what the competitors were up to, and had personal knowledge about the corporate managements and boards, in part because the investment bankers performing due diligence in advance of underwritings shared what they had learned with the analysts. Some of these investment bankers golfed regularly with company executives and were privy to the minutest details of an operation. Even Blodget, in his heyday, had made some remarkable predictions that benefitted investors, most notably involving Amazon. He was an early booster of the company, and investors had benefitted from his advice—which Merrill provided free to customers. Other firms similarly provided their analyst reports to their clients. Now the analysts were delinked from the investment bankers. Not only that, the research departments now would have to become self-sustaining.

But the analysts generated little to no money for their firms. Clients were not willing to buy what once had come to them for free.

The quantitative analysts at the proprietary trading desks of banks and big investment banking firms, on the other hand, were making huge profits. And they didn't care an iota about fundamentals. Firms ditched their analysts and invested in their HFT desks. Spitzer didn't realize it at the time, but he was altering a relationship in the markets that would contribute to the violence of the decline on May 6, 2010.

In short, the retail client had to perform his own fundamental research, and this was no easy chore. It required time, patience, and constant attention. An asset manager said, "Not enough of these people are doing the work. They are relying on things like social networks and chat rooms where they get sound bites instead of detailed fundamental analysis. This is a fundamental change in the markets."

Jeff Engelberg, a principal and senior trader at Southeastern Asset Management, told the SEC at a hearing on June 22, 2010, "Our belief is that over time, across market participants, average holding periods have plummeted, and the number of active strategies requiring little or no fundamental knowledge of underlying securities has significantly increased. As a result, whether via prior-placed stop order losses or the real-time panic closure of positions, many market participants did not know what business they fundamentally owned. This ignorance made a bad situation dramatically worse."

This mirrored the panic in the credit markets in 2007 when big banks realized they were holding mortgage securities whose fundamentals they did not at all understand and therefore could not value. Instruments once considered treasure had turned to dross. Banks and brokerage houses had bought the mortgage securities because everyone else was buying them. They relied on rating agencies for due diligence instead of kicking the tires themselves. A trader profiled by Michael Lewis in *The Big Short* recalled, "It was like watching an unthinking machine that could not stop itself."[4]

Wall Street had learned little from the credit default fiasco that had been triggered by the mortgage market crash. The unthinking machine was still running, but this time at run-away speed.

Endnotes

1. Scott Patterson, "Fast Traders' New Edge," *The Wall Street Journal*, June 4, 2010.

2. Andrew Serwer, "They're Mad as Hell at the Market...But There Isn't Much Investors Can Do About It," *Fortune*, April 2, 2001.

3. Marcia Vickers and Mike France, "How Corrupt Is Wall Street?," *Bloomberg Businessweek*, May 13, 2002.

4. Michael Lewis, *The Big Short*, New York: W.W. Norton & Co., 2010, Kindle Edition. Location 2381–2386.

19

The Vigilantes

The problem the Securities and Exchange Commission (SEC) faced in 2010 was that, until it had data from all of the exchanges and other trading centers with order-routing histories, it would not be able to make up its mind whether high-frequency trading (HFT) was benevolent or evil. The SEC was in the process of collecting that hard data, but the process was taking months. Also, the agency did not have computing power to crunch the numbers on its own. It planned to build such a system, but in the summer of 2010, it had to rely in the exchanges for this, too. And the exchanges were the proverbial foxes guarding the henhouse.

Connaughton, Senator Kaufman's right-hand man, railed, "You've got to open the circle somehow. You've got to get more objective analysis. And the only way you can do that is by collecting the data and putting it out to people on a time-delayed basis." This was a Wiki-world approach, where academics and computer geeks could add their 2 cents of wisdom. It was an approach alien to a federal bureaucracy long schooled in the ways of jealously guarding its turf.

The SEC was approaching the issues surrounding the Flash Crash and HFT in run-of-the-mill fashion. The agency set in motion a rule-making process—a long-drawn-out, exercise that in the past had taken up to three years to complete as the regulators struggled to build a consensus among hostile parties. In these rulemakings, the SEC tended to be overly reliant on soft data—comments from the public and the industry—an approach that reflected the out-sized influence of lawyers at the agency. The end, jury-rigged result, which reflected competing interests, hardly ever resulted in improved markets bit in more complicated markets.

Connaughton had told SEC staff as early as January, at the beginning of the lengthy opinion-gathering process, "I can tell you right now that 98% of the comments coming back from the concept release will be from people telling you that everything is great." And this was the way the process had played out. Joan C. Conley, senior vice president and corporate secretary at NASDAQ OMX, a major stock exchange, sent the commission a typical industry submission on April 30, the week prior to the Flash Crash: "NASDAQ OMX markets and investors have benefited from the Commission's policy to let 'a thousand flowers bloom.' Over 200 market centers now report execution and routing quality statistical reports, and a dozen exchanges contribute to the public reference prices. Market structure will serve investors best by ensuring the broadest possible mix of participants rather than attempting to rank or otherwise elevate some investors over others. The open interaction of diverse trading interests and strategies—whether long term, short term, retail, institutional, or proprietary—promotes continued innovation and efficiency. Vilifying or excluding entire sets of market participants, such as high-speed automated traders, undermines historical Commission policies favoring competition."

The same day, the SEC received a comment letter from James J. Angel, Ph.D., CFA, and associate professor of finance at Georgetown University McDonough School of Business: "The equity market structure is working better than ever, so don't mess it up." He did suggest presciently that the market might need "high-frequency circuit breakers," those statistical trip wires intended to stop trading in a particular stock that was rising or falling with unusual rapidity.

The SEC may not have changed with the times, but the world had changed, owing to the Internet. The SEC no longer was able to exert enough centrifugal force to maintain itself at the center of the heated debate on market structure, let alone control it. The Internet democratized the process. Thousands of arm-chair critics had bloomed. What's more, a number of events transpired to keep May 6 prominently in front of a public reputed to have a short attention span. There was a series of mini-flash crashes in individual stocks. One June 2, 2010, shares of Diebold, the maker of automatic teller machines, plummeted 35% in 1 minute, from $28 per share to $18 per share, and then they snapped right snapped back. Three minutes later, news outlets began reporting that Diebold had made good on a previously announced agreement with the SEC to pay a $25 million fine to settle charges that it had inflated its earnings between 2002 and 2007. The weird, lightning-quick price move smelled of insider trading. Kaufman went to the Senate floor to demand an investigation and in doing so brought the micro-crash to the attention of the baying hounds of the press.

"The SEC should investigate both the manner in which the news broke and the trading activity that followed it," he said. "The SEC was actually resolving an old investigation with Diebold, the settlement of which had been previously disclosed, and not making any new accusations against the company. But when word of the complaint reached Bloomberg or other sources, it led to a *trigger* that potentially activated algorithms programmed to react immediately to breaking news. This may explain why trading activity in Diebold exploded shortly before the story broke publicly."

Regulators, he said, should examine whether the precipitous drop in Diebold stock was the result of a glitch in trading algorithms used by high-frequency traders to respond to breaking news.

This sort of algorithm had been available for years. Reuters had been hawking a system to algorithmic traders that allowed their machines to "read" news articles and to score the degree to which the stories were either positive or negative for a particular security or the market in general. Reuter's advertised, "The system will enable customers to analyze news across thousands of companies, far more quickly than can be done by humans. This will enable trading machines to react to market moving news in milliseconds." Dow Jones was selling 20 years' worth of financial news data to enable traders to write algorithms that let their machines see how past news events had impacted the markets and specific stocks so that the machines could make predictions about effect of similar news stories as they occurred in the future.

Aware of all this, Kaufman admonished the SEC in his floor speech, "With so much of the marketplace dominated by high-frequency traders employing similar strategies, an overreaction by a few algorithms looking to trade instantaneously on the basis of imprecise correlations could trigger a dramatic plunge. Regulators should add to their list the need to examine whether the precipitous drop in Diebold stock was the result of high-frequency traders who can subscribe directly to market data and news feeds and perhaps had programmed faulty correlations into their algorithms to react to breaking news events."

Then on June 16, three orders totaling 766 shares pushed shares of the *Washington Post* up 99% in one second, from $462.84 to $929.18. This was yet another public embarrassment for the SEC and the exchanges.

Kaufman's ire was raised a notch the same month with news that the giant HFT firm Getco had hired the SEC's Elizabeth King as a member of its regulatory affairs team. King was an associate director in the SEC's division of trading and markets and ostensibly involved in its study of HFT issues. He took to the Senate floor again.

Kaufman said, "This is another example of regulatory capture at its worst. It is one thing for Wall Street firms to hire SEC staff for their general knowledge and expertise. It is quite another, however, when the leading HFT firm, Getco, reaches into the SEC's Division of Trading and Markets and hires a senior official who presumably has been close to, or perhaps substantially involved in, a major ongoing Commission review of a broad range of market structure and HFT issues in the equity markets—a review that should lead to additional rule-makings that will have a direct bearing on Getco's trading strategies."

The speech engendered more negative headlines for the HFT industry. It also caught the eye of Iowa Senator Charles Grassley, the ranking Republican on the finance committee. Grassley had been a long-time critic of government regulators and Capitol Hill staff who used their positions to land better-paying jobs with the private-sector companies under their purview. He fired off a letter to the SEC's inspector general David Kotz requesting an investigation into the "revolving door" at the agency. He cited an article in the April 5, 2010, *Wall Street Journal* that reported numerous instances in which an SEC employee had left and represented clients before the commission only days later. Reporter Tom McGinty had found that lower-level employees of the commission could legally appear at the SEC on behalf of clients the day after they had left their agency jobs, as long as they had filed letters of disclosure.

Kotz told Grassley he was investigating the matter, which caused another flurry of negative headlines about the SEC and its investigation of the HFT phenomenon.

McGinty had quoted John P. Freeman, a former SEC lawyer and professor of professional and business ethics at the University of South Carolina School of Law, whose own research documented the high proportion of SEC employees who went on to work for the industries they had once policed.

"The training and expertise gained at the SEC is put to use for the benefit of those working against the interests of investors," Mr. Freeman said.

Around the same time, FIA Principal Traders Group, a group quickly created by the Futures Industry Association to help shape press coverage of high-frequency traders, contracted former SEC Chief Economist James Overdahl as its spokesman. Mr. Overdahl had worked for the SEC from July 2007 to March, 31, 2010. He had left to join an economic consulting firm in Washington, DC. His new role, though perfectly legal, was the source of more negative stories about regulators being cozy with the HFT industry.

The SEC was beginning to feel some heat. Chairman Schapiro had told international regulators at a June 10, 2010 meeting in Montreal that her agency needed to "explore whether bids and orders should be regulated on speed so there is less incentive to engage in this microsecond arms race that might undermine long-term investors and the market's capital-formation function." Of course, there was a significant difference between "exploring" and "acting." Kaufman wanted the SEC to aggressively police the high-frequency sector, which was pretty much untamed territory. His mantra was, "If you can't regulate it and it's not transparent and there's lots of money involved, then it is going to blow up."

Kaufman was a short-timer. His term expired at the end of 2010. The SEC could drag things out for years.

"I think a lot of the things Schapiro says make sense, and that she's genuinely interested in doing it. But there's this desire for consensus. You're not going to get consensus with these guys. If I'm making a billion dollars a year and you want to change things so I don't make a billion dollars anymore, then you're never going to get me to sign off on that," Kaufman said.[1]

He wondered how to give Schapiro one final, effective push. He was only asking for transparency for that sector of the market in the form of increased reporting by HFT and better monitoring of market activity by the SEC, not a major addition to the regulatory canon. And the sooner the light of day shone on the high-frequency traders' corner of the market, the better. But the SEC was moving at glacial speed. The word *alacrity* seemed missing from the SEC's vocabulary. Then the proverbial cavalry rode to Kaufman's rescue.

Endnotes

1. Interview with author, September 2010.

20

The Tide Turns

Eric Scott Hunsader, a man who few on Wall Street or in Washington, DC, had ever heard of, helped change the tenor of the debate on high-frequency trading (HFT) with a sensational charge in June 2010 that was picked up by major news media. Hunsader, a self-made software and stock market expert, and Jeffrey Donovan, one of his company's software engineers, had analyzed trading data for May 6 across all the markets and exchanges and concluded that traders had deliberately slowed the consolidated tape that fateful day by flooding it with thousands of orders minutes before the Flash Crash occurred, possibly causing the dramatic dislocation. Further research by Hunsader indicated the traders played this game on a daily basis so they could profit from the price discrepancies that resulted among the many exchanges from the manipulation of tape. It was a sensational charge. It was so sensational, in fact, that the SEC's regulators were highly skeptical of their veracity. However, one element of Hunsader's claim was found to be accurate: The consolidated tape had slowed considerably on May 6—by as much as 35 seconds. Neither the regulators nor the exchanges had noticed this before Hunsader brought it to their attention. Although the rest of his charges seemed fantastic, the regulators could not dismiss Hunsader's theories out of hand because the slowdown had been real.

The consolidated tape displayed pricing information from the individual exchanges to the broader market. Retail investors relied on the tape to set buying and selling prices for stocks. High-frequency traders, on the other hand, subscribed to direct feeds from each exchange and saw prices before they were posted to the consolidated tape. The Securities and Exchange Commission (SEC) believed the time advantage for the traders was about 1 millisecond. Hunsader said his data showed it was, in fact, hundreds of milliseconds. If the traders had advanced knowledge of the market's direction and a head start in employing that knowledge, they could make more money than investors relying on slower data feed. Theoretically, a high-frequency trader could short a stock before the general public caught wind that it was headed lower, or the trader might snap up shares that were headed higher, before the move became evident on the tape.

Hunsader claimed the traders, several times each day, were sending quotes for a Big Board stock or combination of stocks to an exchange at the rate of 20,000 quotes per second versus a usual flow rate of about 10,000 quotes per second. The higher or longer the message traffic stayed above 20,000 quotes per second, the slower the tape. Hunsader called the strategy *quote-stuffing*, and it immediately fired the imagination of a public distrustful of the stock market.

His data showed that on April 28, 2010, quote stuffers had triggered an ultra-mini flash crash in a number of stocks like Procter & Gamble and Wal-Mart, which fell by 50 cents and then fully recovered in just two seconds—more than enough time for a high-frequency trader to short the stocks, buy in at the low, and then sell when they again traded with a normal bid-ask spread of a cent. "It was eerily similar to May 6," he asserted.[1]

Hunsader was the founder of a small company called Nanex, located in Winnetka, IL, a suburb of Chicago. The company collected trade and quote data from equities, options, futures, futures options, and other exchanges, normalized it, compressed it by a factor of 20 to one and delivered it over the internet worldwide to the personal computers of its subscribers, who he said were largely institutional and retail traders.

Hunsader began his stock market career after graduating from Wake Forest University in 1984. The Bradenton, Florida resident had intended to become a physician, but when he walked out of an interview at what was then known as the Bowman Gray School of Medicine, he had an epiphany. He did not really want to become a doctor. He decided instead to try his hand at day trading.

This, of course, was in the midst of the Reagan bull market, which had started in the second quarter of 1982. The Dow Jones Industrial Average (DJIA) was headed higher in 1984 following a slight retreat the previous year. Hunsader had saved $6,000 while attending college. He boldly took $4,000 and purchased a top-of-the-line IBM PC. He subscribed to a quote system and traded S&P 500 futures. He ended the year with $5,000 in profits and bought a second computer.

Hunsader soon became bored with trading. One had to follow strict rules to be successful, and the activity did not appeal to his creative side. So in 1985, he went to the local book store, picked up a manual on C programming language, and devoured it. Hunsader quickly became proficient in this version of computer language. He wrote a program to collect data from the Chicago Mercantile Exchange (CME) and post it to a bulletin board accessible to PCs linked to the Internet. Then he launched his own company to sell the bulletin-board service. He later sold it at a handsome profit. A version of the service was still being sold in 2010, which was a testimonial to its enduring usefulness.

Hunsader married and moved to Illinois because he and his wife considered it an ideal place to raise a family. It was also an ideal location for his next venture, Nanex, because it was proximate to the futures market.

Hunsader posted his analysis of the Flash Crash on his company's Web site on June 24, 2010, for the edification of his subscribers. Word of the study spread like wildfire. In short, it went "viral," which means that its contents spread to other Web sites and was a hot topic of discussion among bloggers. Andrei Kirilenko, a senior financial economist at the Commodities Futures Trading Commission

(CFTC), visited the site to see what the hoopla was about and was intrigued enough by Hunsader's research to invite the programmer to discuss his findings at a July 8 seminar at CFTC headquarters.

Hunsader expected the presentation to last just an hour or so, but the CFTC kept him for the entire day. His discussion with more than 100 CFTC staff was multicast to CFTC regional offices in several cities. He detailed his research and recommended that the regulators obtain further data from the exchanges to confirm his quote-stuffing theory. Hunsader capped the visit by briefing CFTC Commissioner Scott O' Malia for 45 minutes. O'Malia chaired an advisory panel on technological issues.

The CFTC, in turn, sent one of their programmers to Nanex for two days to learn to manipulate its data. Hunsader had convinced them it was theoretically possible for algorithmic traders to slow down the consolidated tape. They wanted to crunch his numbers themselves before concluding it did in fact happen on May 6 and other days.

The CFTC staff was so impressed with Hunsader's presentation that it encouraged the SEC staff to interview him. But the SEC staff was lukewarm to the recommendation. In their minds, a sensational charge required sensational evidence, and they just didn't see it in the Nanex data. One reason the tapes had slowed was because the New York Stock Exchange (NYSE) had been updating feeds for about half its listed stocks the day of the crash. Three SEC representatives had attended the CFTC event to listen to Hunsader, and they had not been overly impressed. "We'll get around to it," was the response that the CFTC heard.[2]

The SEC staff was so focused on finding a smoking gun to explain the Flash Crash that they missed the import of Hunsader's charges. He was telling them that the markets were being manipulated by quote stuffing every day. And their reaction was, "What does this have to do with May 6? Did quote stuffing cause the market to crash?"[3] This irked the CFTC staff members, who believed that quote stuffing was theoretically possible.

The SEC staff had other reasons for its skepticism. The NYSE could not duplicate Hunsader's findings, and the SEC's regulators were more inclined to believe the exchanges than some self-proclaimed "expert" who had come out of left field. Hunsader was a new face—a completely unknown face. This made the SEC staff highly uncomfortable. They were also hearing from MIT-educated physicists and mathematicians at HFT firms who were deriding Hunsader's theories as crackpot. They asked rhetorically, "How could any serious expert use data from the consolidated tape for a scientifically sound study?" The tape's data was untrustworthy, they argued. The only good data was that provided by direct feeds from the exchanges to subscribers like the HFT firms. If Hunsader had analyzed that data and had found something amiss, he'd be more credible, they argued. They also contended that there were other, more rational explanations for the surge in trading from time to time throughout the day. Some HFT firms might be testing new strategies, using bids and offers away from the prevailing best bid and best offer because they didn't want the test orders to be filled. Some high-frequency traders might be testing the latencies of their computers by continually sending orders to the exchanges that have no hope of being filled to see how long it takes to receive an order.

Unlike the staff at the SEC, the CFTC staff wasn't swayed by these arguments. In their view, it didn't matter if there *was* quote stuffing. What mattered was that quote stuffing appeared to be a theoretical possibility, and if it was theoretically possible, there was a serious flaw in the market's structure that should be addressed. The CFTC staff was irked by the SEC's seeming indifference—so irked, in fact, that it threatened to investigate on its own if the SEC would not do it. That would not have looked good for either agency. The friction would have generated calling into question the credibility of the "joint" investigation. The equities market was the SEC's turf. The press would play it up as a Hatfield-versus-McCoy-style feud, with the CFTC accusing the SEC of a lack of diligence.

The SEC invited Hunsader to its headquarters for an hour and a half on July 19, 2010. The staff members were polite, but Hunsader sensed they did not appreciate his message.

Hunsader later said, "The CFTC really got it. I think if they were in charge of things, then you'd really see things getting done."

He sized up the SEC as being "afraid to be the parent."

"They don't need to create new rules to rein this in. All they have to do is enforce Regulation NMS, which they spent God knows how many tax dollars creating. Blatant violations occur all of the time, and either they really don't understand or they do and are getting such push-back from the exchanges that they are afraid to do anything about it."

About this time, the CFTC staff approached members of the Senate and House Agricultural Committees and convinced the lawmakers to slip Section 747 into the Dodd-Frank Act so they at least could regulate HFT on the commodities exchanges. While Schapiro and her team waffled, Gensler and his team were busy supplanting the SEC as the leading market regulator.

In August, knowledge of Hunsader's data was brought to the world at large by *The Atlantic* magazine. There were follow-up stories in *The New York Times*, *Barron's*, and *The Wall Street Journal*. And CFTC Commissioner Bart Chilton at a public meeting of the CFTC-SEC joint committee on August 11 kept the issue alive by urging the panel to look more closely at the possibility that high-frequency traders were taking advantage of time delays in the consolidated tape.

"I'm not convinced we have looked at this enough yet," he said afterwards. "Did they instigate the time difference and take advantage of it? If they instigated it, then it would be a really big deal."

Hunsader's credibility was growing. HFT advocates had been claiming they brought only good to the market. Hunsader's data apparently showed otherwise. And he seemed to be on the ball. Hunsader had conducted the sort of research that the SEC should have done for the preliminary report on the Flash Crash.

The SEC's credibility, on the other hand, was shrinking. The fact that the owner of a small company was able to produce data that had showed a slowing of the consolidated tape while the SEC could not because of a lack of technology simply astounded the public. This was a major embarrassment for the agency, which considered itself the market's cop. Now the world knew the SEC was blind as a bat. How would Mary Schapiro's SEC ever be able to restore investor confidence in the market if it lacked the basic tools required to get to the root of the market's problem?

Endnotes

1. Jim McTague, "Was the Flash Crash Rigged?," *Barron's Magazine*. August 30, 2010.

2. Author interview with a confidential source within the CFTC.

3. Author interview with Eric Scott Hunsader, August 24, 2010.

21

Letter Bomb

When Michael Cembalest talked about the market, people paid close attention. The chief investment officer at JP Morgan Private Bank oversaw close to $1 trillion in investments. His opinion mattered. So when he was highly critical of certain aspects of high-frequency trading (HFT) in his biweekly "Eye on the Market" letter to his clients on July 13, 2010, it caused a sensation on Wall Street and in Washington, DC, as well.

Cembalest asserted that HFT was eroding confidence in the equities market and that the Securities and Exchange Commission (SEC) needed to take immediate steps to correct this disturbing trend.

Jim Cramer, the animated host of CNBC's popular *Mad Money* show, got a copy of the letter and discussed it at length on his program. Another copy of the letter was posted on the Internet and, like Hunsader's quote-stuffing study, it went "viral." Cembalest became an overnight sensation because he dared to say what others in the industry believed but were reluctant to utter: Investor flights from U.S. equity funds were a direct result of the Flash Crash and HFT.

At the time Cembalest had written his letter, retail investors had been withdrawing cash from domestic equity mutual funds for 18 consecutive weeks. This was a run on the stock market, and Cembalest was startled by it.

High-frequency traders had been arguing vociferously that their industry stood for progress and that progress was a net positive for the market. Cembalest responded to this argument by writing, "There's a postmodern temptation to define all forms of innovation as progress, but there are big differences between the two. One example: While some forms of genetic engineering are possible, they may also be very undesirable. The downside to some innovation only becomes apparent over time (overuse of antibiotics which may lead to the survival of more virulent strains of bacteria; species transplantation that cause disastrous side-effects for local populations). Some derivatives activity (e.g., CDO-cubed) ended up being innovations with strongly negative aftershocks. You do not have to be a Luddite to raise questions about undesired consequences of innovation, particularly when financial services are involved. The debate is not about reversing innovation in electronic trading, but making adjustments along the way."

Certainly, high-frequency traders had lowered spreads and other trading costs. But in Cembalest's view, these savings were offset by hidden costs. He cited a study that estimated HFT tracking algorithms were increasing execution costs for institutional traders by 1.5 to 3 times.

Cembalest saw a demographic change taking place that would increase savings rates in the United States up to 7% percent, the highest levels in more than 25 years. If the United States wanted a vibrant capital market, it had to attract some of that savings to the equities. Cembalest believed it might be good policy to trade some of the pricing efficiency gained by decimalization and increased automation by opting for a market with deeper liquidity, stability, and a sense of fair play. Otherwise, this money would remain on the sidelines.

"How do you mobilize America's savings so the Federal Reserve no longer has to do the heavy lifting? The stakes are very high here," he said.

Kaufman kept up the pressure about HFT, too. On August 5, 2010, he sent Schapiro a letter slamming the agency for foot-dragging. He said that the SEC and Financial Industry Regulatory Authority (FINRA) had to put a stop to the "wild west environment" of the HFT world and actively police that corner of the market for illicit trading. He also suggested that the SEC prohibit high-frequency traders from getting prices ahead of the consolidated tape.

At the rate the SEC was moving, it might take as long as three years to address the problems decried by Kaufman. In the meantime, investors were beginning to doubt the stability and fairness of the equity market.

"If the Commission has the will, there is indeed a way to do this faster," Kaufman challenged.

The chatter about the letter and the public's loss of confidence in the market since the Flash Crash became pervasive—so much so that it was a topic the regulators could hardly ignore. Not only was the public's withdrawal from the market a bad omen for the economy, it was bad for Schapiro and Gensler's political patron, President Barack Obama, whose popularity was sliding because of a national unemployment rate of 9.5%.

Schapiro's political and finely tuned instincts kicked in immediately. Under visible pressure from the media and from Kaufman, she finally began to appreciate the dimensions of the crisis spawned by the Flash Crash. The day after the Labor Day holiday weekend, when the press was hungry for news, Schapiro delivered a speech to the New York Economic Club sounding a new Flash Crash theme. The market, she emphasized for the first time, was designed primarily for capital formation. It was a vital engine of economic growth.

"Our markets have a profound impact on the rate at which our economy grows and creates jobs. And, they have an impact on the welfare of millions of individual Americans looking to save for college or their retirement," she said. She noted that when the stock market breaks down, investors pull back, increasing costs for companies and reducing growth. Evidence indicated that the markets indeed seemed to have broken down. Retail investors had pulled money from equity mutual funds every week since the Flash Crash.

Kaufman and Connaughton were overjoyed by the speech. Schapiro finally was speaking out for long-term investors.

Schapiro concluded that day, "The important questions are to what extent is our structure meeting or failing to meet its goals of fair, efficient, and transparent markets, and how can we modify the structure to preserve the advantages and eliminate the flaws? Answering these questions will not be easy, but I do know this: Hard and careful work to strengthen our equity market structure will bring important dividends to investors, companies, and the economy as a whole."

But when would she take some action?

Six days later, FINRA, the industry-financed regulator of brokerage firms, announced large fines and suspensions against principals and employees of Trillium Brokerage Services LLC to settle charges of illicit HFT on 46,000 occasions between November 1, 2006 and January 31, 2007. Although the case was hardly fresh, it had symbolic significance. The regulators were declaring to the politicians, to the public, and to the markets that they were on top of the HFT situation intended to crack the whip. They were telling Congress that they had heard its concerns about high-frequency traders and were taking them seriously. It was a grand illusion, but no one in the traditional business press caught on. Trillium was one of the last of the old-fashioned day-trading firms, not an HFT firm. And its alleged sins involved human players trying to outsmart the machines of other automated traders in a rather old-fashioned way called *layering*. FINRA was like a police department that had caught some bicycle thieves and bumped up the charge to grand theft auto to make their crime-fighting statistics look more attractive.

FINRA had begun looking at Trillium's records in January 2010. Six months later, in July, the case was ready to be made. But regulators wanted to wait for a golden moment when the announcement would have maximum impact. So they waited until after Labor Day, the traditional start of the campaign season. At the time, it already was evident that Democrats were facing a disaster on November 2 because of the party's failure to revive the economy. And, in fact, they did. Democrats managed to hang on in the Senate, where the GOP picked up six seats. But the Democrats lost 61 seats in the House as well as losing control of the chamber.

Popular Reuters financial blogger Felix Salmon, a market expert, saw through the Trillium charade immediately. He wrote, "What Trillium did is market manipulation, to be sure, and it deserves a fine. But it's a bit of a stretch to paint this as the first battle in the war against high-frequency traders—not least because there isn't actually anything particularly high frequency about what Trillium was doing. Yes, FINRA does say that Trillium's layering was an "improper high-frequency trading strategy." But fundamentally it was about misdirection, rather than speed."[1]

Layering was a straightforward scam. Salmon offered an example of XYZ stock trading at a bid of $24.50 and an offer of $24.55. A trader who wants to sell her shares simply might hit the bid and receive $24.50; or she could chose instead to put in a sell order at $24.54 and hope that someone wanting to buy will take her out there. Salmon said that would be the better outcome because the trader would get a better price plus a small rebate from the exchange for acting as a "liquidity provider." The downside is that there might not be a buyer at that price.

Now, if that trader is a conniver, she might place a hidden offer at $24.54, in a dark pool, which is legal. This means that the offer is there, but no one in the public or "lit" markets can see it. Then comes what Salmon described as *the sneaky part*: The trader puts in a large number of public and visible *bids* at prices like $24.48 and $24.47. Remember, she wants to sell XYZ, not buy more shares. She's trying to make it look like there is a large amount of buying interest building in XYZ, knowing that any electronic trading algorithm will look at the size of the bid and the size of the ask to determine the *depth of the order book* or, simply, the amount of visible supply and the amount of visible demand. A naively designed algorithm will fall for the ploy.

"So they start putting in their own bids: at $24.51, $24.52, $24.53. They're all trying to get in front of the big new buyer they see in the market. And presto, when they bid $24.54, they find that hidden sell order from Trillium, which gets a very good price on its trade *and* gets to count as a liquidity provider. And as soon as that happens, all those fake bids at $24.48 and $24.47 suddenly disappear. But the victims are the people (or algorithms) who thought there was a naive trader posting public buy orders and wanted to trade against that order," explained Salmon.[2]

High-frequency traders had been Trillium's victims, but FINRA was making it look like high-frequency traders had been the victimizers. There was more show than substance to the action. And FINRA had to coordinate its announcement with the SEC. It made people begin to doubt Schapiro's sincerity.

Endnotes

1. Felix Salmon, "Trillium Wasn't Quote Stuffing," blogs.reuters.com, September 14, 2010.

2. Ibid.

22

Scapegoat

The Commodities Futures Trading Commission (CFTC) and Securities and Exchange Commission (SEC) issued its long-awaited report on the Flash Crash on Friday, October 1, 2010, and it landed with a thud. Titled "Findings Regarding the Market Events of May 6, 2010" and subtitled "Report of the Staffs of the CFTC and SEC to the Joint Advisory Commission on Regulatory Issues," its explanation of the crash in the executive summary heaped blame on one party while ladling gentle teaspoons of blame on others who were far more culpable. Few news reports got beyond these opening pages, so their stories uncritically repeated the slanted story that a single large and reckless trade by a "mutual fund complex" had been the event that triggered the massive selloff on May 6. Case closed. The market once again was safe for widows and orphans.

But the SEC's narrative upon closer scrutiny did not hold up beyond a reasonable doubt. The agency's thesis was as ludicrous as the press report that blamed the Great Chicago Fire of 1871 on Catherine O'Leary's cow rather than on the city's faulty building codes and its defective fire alarm system. The market structure on May 6, 2010 simply did not function the way it was supposed to function when under pressure from a wave of selling. The regulators had erected a shaky edifice and were loath to admit it. They had looked everywhere for a scapegoat but in the one place the real culprit was to be found: the mirror. So they ended up pinning the blame on a company identified by the press as Waddell & Reed, Overland Park, Kansas.

Asked by a Reuter's reporter two days earlier how she thought the public would respond to the findings, SEC Chairman Schapiro responded, "I think they will feel confident, and they'll feel confident that the SEC and the CFTC staffs have a very deep understanding of the markets as a result of this inquiry, and that we have some ideas on how to go forward."

She must have had her fingers crossed that this would prove so: The retail investor was still on the sidelines despite the fact that September proved to be the single strongest monthly gain in the Standard & Poor's (S&P) 500 in 71 years. Total stock market volume was off a whopping 25% in the third quarter, which had bled earnings at the exchanges. Wall Street badly needed a boost. Schapiro obviously thought that the report would do the trick. She was wrong. The market remained volatile. Traders still dominated the action. Under these circumstances, the SEC's report hardly was reassuring. The October 4, 2010 headline in *USA TODAY* read "Flash Crash Mystery Solved But No Fixes Suggested." Reporter Adam Shell opined, "The reason for the lukewarm response to the report on the May 6 *flash crash*, released Friday by the Securities and Exchange Commission and Commodity Futures Trading Commission is that it focuses solely on answering one question: What happened? What the report doesn't do: Outline a plan to fix the market's structural flaws. The omission was glaring, as investors' mistrust of the market remains high."

The regulators, even those who had been critical of the investigation's conduct, displayed unity in the face of this public skepticism.

"We're better off today than we were," said the CFTC's Chilton. The SEC had adopted circuit breakers, and although he admitted that this step more or less was a "band-aid approach," he argued on television that the action was sufficient enough to prevent another Flash Crash.

But was the investing public really better off? The meat of the Flash Crash report—the jargon-encrusted chapters that lay behind the executive summary—painted a much grimmer picture of the condition of the market on the day of the meltdown. The public and the press hadn't caught on because the mumbo jumbo was difficult for them to comprehend. It was almost as if the bureaucrats had deliberately downplayed the role of other market constituencies in the sharp collapse of prices. A careful reading of the report revealed that the actions of brokerage firms and high-frequency traders had fanned the fires of panic more than the attempt by Waddell & Reed to hedge its stock portfolio.

The report imputed that the Waddell & Reed trade had been flawed on a number of levels. The company, it said, employed the wrong kind of algorithm, one that dumped too many shares into the market too quickly, which was an error considering the level of panic and the thinning of liquidity in E-Mini futures contracts. The order size, the report stated, was 75,000 E-Mini contracts valued at $4.1 billion.

"Generally, a customer has a number of alternatives as to how to execute a large trade," the report noted. "First, a customer may choose to engage an intermediary, who would, in turn, execute a block trade or manage the position. Second, a customer may choose to manually enter orders into the market. Third, a customer can execute a trade via an automated execution algorithm, which can meet the customer's needs by taking price, time, or volume into consideration. Effectively, a customer must make a choice as to how much human judgment is involved while executing a trade."

"This large fundamental trader chose to execute this sell program via an automated execution algorithm ("Sell Algorithm") that was programmed to feed orders into the June 2010 E-Mini market to target an execution rate set to 9% of the trading volume calculated over the previous minute, but without regard to price or time."

"The execution of this sell program resulted in the largest net change in daily position of any trader in the E-Mini since the beginning of the year (from January 1, 2010 through May 6, 2010). Only two, single-day sell programs of equal or larger size—one of which was by the same large fundamental trader—were executed in the E-Mini in the 12 months prior to May 6. When executing the previous sell program, this large fundamental trader utilized a combination of manual trading entered over the course of a day and several auto-mated execution algorithms which took into account price, time, and volume. On that occasion it took more than 5 hours for this large trader to execute the first 75,000 contracts of a large sell program."

"However, on May 6, when markets were already under stress, the sell algorithm chosen by the large trader to only target trading volume, and neither price nor time, executed the sell program extremely rapidly in just 20 minutes."[1]

"In essence, once the $4.1 billion order was entered into the algo-rithm, it was as if it was on auto-pilot in an otherwise fragile market," CFTC Chairman Gensler said in a speech on October 4, 2010.

HFT firms were only too happy with the regulator's choice of a scapegoat because they felt they had been exonerated of complicity in the Flash Crash. David Cummings, owner and chairman of Tradebot Systems Inc, an HFT firm, sent out a screed via e-mail headlined "Waddell Stupidity Caused Crash." Cummings wrote, "Wow! Who puts in a $4.1 billion order without a limit price? The trader at Waddell & Reed showed historic incompetence."

There was another side to the story, however, and it cast serious doubt on the accuracy of the joint report. In the first place, Waddell & Reed's trade was neither unusual nor unusually large. The Chicago Mercantile Exchange (CME) made this clear in an October 1 press release: "The report references a series of *bona fide* hedging transac-tions, totaling 75,000 contracts, entered into by an institutional asset manager to hedge a portion of the risk in its $75 billion investment portfolio in response to global economic events and the fundamen-tally deteriorating market conditions that day. The 75,000 contracts represented 1.3% of the total E-Mini volume of 5.7 million contracts on May 6 and less than 9% of the volume during the time period in which the orders were executed. The prevailing market sentiment was evident well before these orders were placed, and the orders, as well as the manner in which they were entered, *were both legitimate and consistent with market practices.* These hedging orders were entered *in relatively small quantities* and in a manner designed to dynamically adapt to market liquidity by participating in a target percentage of 9% of the volume executed in the market. As a result of the significant volumes traded in the market, the hedge was completed in approximately twenty minutes, with more than half of the participant's volume executed as the market rallied—not as the market declined. Additionally, the aggregate size of this participant's orders was not known to other market participants."

In other words, none of the E-Mini traders could be panicked by a large order because there was no way of knowing there was a large order. Waddell & Reed didn't advertise that it had 75,000 contracts for sale. The market is anonymous. Buyers and sellers didn't see a large seller but merely continuous action. And, in the second place, the company didn't dump the large order into the market as the report said it did. The algorithm, which was designed to mimic the action of a human trader, made certain that the order represented 9 out of every 100 trades. Only 35,000 of the trades had entered the E-Mini market during the 20 minutes of decline, half of the order.

Other traders were selling E-Minis at the same time. So placing the entire blame on Waddell & Reed was misleading.

"This firm is being demonized—and it's part of a game of deception," fumed Arnuk of Themis Trading.

According to the report's authors, the mutual funds trader had selected an algorithm from a drop-down menu of algorithmic strategies.[2] Companies like Goldman Sachs and UBS sold suites of algorithms to mutual funds and told them that the programs would allow them to execute trades without disrupting the markets. Furthermore, the trader had consulted with an executing broker at the exchange who had concurred with the selection of the algorithm. It hadn't been a rash choice.

The CME bills the S&P E-Mini market as one of the most liquid in the world, and this generally is the case. The instrument is traded heavily around the world, 24 hours per day. Yet on May 6, volume in the E-Mini had declined to $58 million by 2:45 p.m., which was less than 1% of the volume that morning (see Figure 22.1). But neither Waddell & Reed nor thousands of other traders were privy to this detailed information. As one wag noted, it took the regulators five months to figure this out. Waddell & Reed had good reason to assume their order would be digested that day.

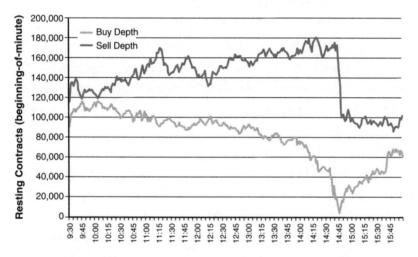

Figure 22.1   E-Mini market depth (all quotes).

Source: CFTC and SEC, May 6, 2010, Market Event Findings

(In any event, displayed liquidity doesn't tell traders much about a market's depth. In times of volatility, market participants reduce their displayed buying and selling interests out of caution. But it doesn't always follow that there is less interest. In October 2008, displayed liquidity in equity index markets was near historic lows. Nevertheless, the exchanges reported peak volume.)

The joint report said that high-frequency traders and other market-making intermediaries probably bought the first batch of sell orders from Waddell & Reed. High-frequency traders accumulated a net long position of 3,300 contracts. At the same time, the report says, high-frequency traders were trading contracts back and fourth among their machines, probably to accumulate rebate. They traded 140,000 contracts, or 33% of the total volume, giving the illusion of a deep pool of buyers. But they got cold feet between 2:41 p.m. and 2:44 p.m. and sold 2,000 of them. They had stopped providing liquidity and began competing for it, and that drove the price of the E-Mini S&P 500 future even lower.

The report suggested that Waddell & Reed should have known that high trading volume doesn't always equate to liquidity, especially during tumultuous trading days. But this was exactly what HFT firms and at least one SEC commissioner had been asserting. HFT claimed they bought when others were selling. Regulators in general had bought into that malarkey, so why not Waddell & Reed? The real scandal was that the vaunted equities market system created by the SEC on the instructions of the Congress had failed miserably. It was overly complex and unstable. And the retail customer was right to be terrified because of the hidden horror story hidden in the report: Retail customers on the day of the Flash Crash had been abandoned by brokerage houses and thrown into the fire.

Endnotes

1. Report of the staffs of the CFTC and SEC to the Joint Advisory Committee on Emerging Issues, "Findings Regarding the Market Events of May 6, 2010," 2.

2. Interview with author.

23

The Real Culprits

On the day of the Flash Crash, the Chicago Mercantile Exchange's (CME's) computers spotted what was occurring and paused trading in the E-Mini market for 5 seconds. Because of that brief halt, the E-Mini market recovered immediately. The real meltdown was yet to come—in the equities markets. The ship that the Securities and Exchange Commission (SEC) had built had splintered the minute it encountered a wind gust. Regulators had driven a spike through the pocketbooks of the old-line specialists and the market makers who had once kept trading orderly, forcing most of them out of business. The many had been punished for the sins of a few.

The regulators had meant well. They had believed that computers would be more efficient, dependable, and honest than humans. The high-frequency traders who had supplanted the human market makers proved on May 6 to be even less reliable. Rather than dousing the flames of panic, they helped spread them from market to market and exchange to exchange with their lightning-fast arbitrage strategies. When the E-Mini S&P 500 dropped on the CME, the high-frequency traders knew that index-based exchange-traded funds (ETFs), as well as the actual 500 stocks that make up the Standard & Poor's (S&P) indexes, shortly would drop in price as well, so they began short selling in the equities markets. This sudden wave of selling heightened the general panic. The high-frequency traders had long claimed to dampen volatility through their provision of liquidity. But on May 6, they became net sellers, draining liquidity from the market. This headlong retreat was reminiscent of the behavior of the old NASDAQ market makers who in 1987 had abandoned their posts and refused to answer their telephones in the face of a tidal wave of selling.

What irony. High-frequency trading (HFT) had evolved from day trading, which had been established in reaction to that sorry 1987 market breakdown. Now high-frequency traders were guilty of the same behavior (see Figure 23.1). The joint report noted that a significant number of HFT firms simply stopped trading altogether. This caused buy-side liquidity in a number of securities and in ETFs to evaporate, causing prices to fall even further—in some instances as low as a penny. Unlike the market makers of yore, HFT firms had no formal obligation to try to stop a selling stampede.

The regulators had discussed the situation at length after the Flash Crash. There was a spirited debate whether or not to impose obligations on HFT firms in return for letting them charge investors slightly wider spreads. Transaction costs would rise, but investors would get a more orderly market.

Theodore Weisberg, the president of Seaport Securities and someone who had been trading for more than 41 years, told Bloomberg television that trading in nickel increments instead of penny increments would be enough to attract dealers back to the equities markets. As a result, investor transaction costs would rise, but they'd be getting more stable markets in return, which was what long-term investors preferred.

HFT firms were not the only source of concern in the joint report, however. One of its most damning indictments was aimed squarely at the "internalizers." The SEC described them as over-the-counter (OTC) market makers and block "positioners"—who handle institutional trades. These were the 200 brokerage houses that regularly transacted customer orders in house. They had abandoned their customers on the day the Flash Crash took the DJIA down over 700 points in just 10 minutes.

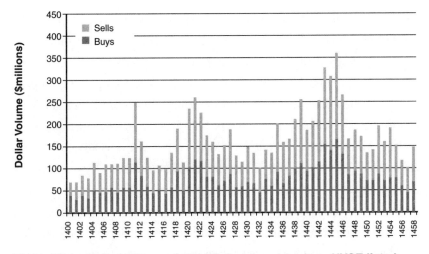

Figure 23.1   Dollar volume of 12 high-frequency traders: NYSE listed (FINRA data set).

Source: CFTC and SEC

The behavior of these brokerage firms on May 6 was one of the biggest outrages in stock market history. Strangely, it wasn't mentioned in the joint report's executive summary. Rather than being highlighted, the tale of their treachery was buried in the back pages of the document.

Internalization on most days accounts for nearly 100% of all retail trades.[1] The practice, authorized by Regulation National Market System (NMS), is a huge profit maker for the firms. They attempt to match one customer's buy or sell order with the buy or sell order of another customer. If the firm can't find a trade that reflects the market's best bid and best offer, it sends it to an executing broker. The executing broker generally takes the opposite side of the customer order because retail customers generally buy high and sell low, so it's easy to make money off of them. In the rare instance when an executing broker demurs, he sends the trade to a dark pool—usually one owned by his firm. If the dark pool can't execute the trade, it is deemed *exhaust* and sent to one of the stock exchanges.

On May 6, some internalizers reduced executions of sell orders but continued to internalize buy orders. In other words, they'd sell stock to a retail customer but would not buy stock from a retail customer. The internalizers were spooked by the wave of selling and wanted to get rid of their own inventories of stock, not accumulate more. So they sent the customer sell orders onto the stock exchanges, which already had more sell orders than they could handle. The report noted, "Other internalizers halted their internalization altogether. Among the rationales for lower rates of internalization were very heavy sell pressure due to retail market and stop-loss orders; an unwillingness to further buy against those sells; data integrity questions due to rapid price moves (and in some cases data latencies); and intraday changes in P&L [profits and losses] that triggered predefined limits. In some instances, when internalizers attempted to route some of their order flow to a dark pool or other internalizer, orders were rebuffed. Partly, this was due to internal systems issues at some entities, and partly this was because each internalizer was experiencing the same events and making the same decisions to reduce or halt internalization. Data on total volume by exchange clearly shows where internalizers and (though not extensively interviewed) dark pools stopped providing liquidity for incoming orders. Internalizers instead routed orders to the exchanges, putting further pressure on the liquidity that remained in those venues."

Many trades that originated from retail customers as stop-loss orders or market orders were converted to limit orders by internalizers prior to routing to the exchanges for execution. A limit order requires the trade to be executed at a specific price, whereas a market order is the best price available at the time an order can be executed. If the limit order wasn't filled because the stock's price had fallen below the designated price level, it was kicked back. The internalizers would then set a new, lower limit price and resubmit the order. The orders were kicked back multiple times because prices were collapsing so rapidly. So these orders followed the prices down, "eventually reaching unrealistically low bids," according to the report.

The executing brokers meant well. Chris Nagy, managing partner for global trading at TD Ameritrade, explained, "In seeking best execution, a broker may use various methods to help ascertain a better price for the client. This tactic is somewhat common to protect unknowing investors from wild price swings, although May 6 was a whole different animal. It's important to note that when this type of strategy is used, it's generally subsecond, and many exchanges don't accept market orders."[2]

Twenty thousand trades of 5.5 million shares that executed 60% or more away from pre-Flash Crash price levels later were broken. According to the report, "one large internalizer (as a seller) and one large market maker (as a buyer) were party to over 50% of the share volume of broken trades, and for more than half of this volume they were counterparties to each other (i.e., 25% of the broken trade share volume was between this particular seller and buyer). Furthermore, in total, data show that internalizers were the sellers for almost half of all broken trade share volume. Given that internalizers generally process and route retail trading interest, this suggests that at least half of all broken trade share volume was due to retail customer sell orders."[3]

The joint report noted, just as Hunsader had established, that the New York Stock Exchange (NYSE) had experienced significant delays in its dissemination of quotes and execution prices to the consolidated tape. Between 2:45 p.m. and 2:50 p.m., reports for 40 out of 1,665 listed stocks were delayed more than 20 seconds. Reports for all 1,665 stocks were delayed more than 5 seconds, with some delays lasting as long as 35 seconds. But the joint report rejected outright Hunsader's thesis that the delays allowed HFT firms with direct pricing feeds from the exchanges to buy securities based on the faster tape and sell them at prices on the slower tape or vice versa.

"It generally is not possible to do this...since the consolidated feeds do not reflect a separate trading market from the exchanges.

One cannot buy or sell at an exchange's prices as shown on the consolidated data feeds separately from the exchange's prices as shown on its proprietary data feed. All orders attempting to execute against an exchange quote in the consolidated data feed must be routed to that exchange where they will be matched on a real-time basis on then-available quotes at that exchange," the authors noted. The joint report added that investors relying on the shorter consolidated tape for pricing information might be in for a surprise because the real-time prices might be quite different. So, in fact, HFT firms had a significant informational jump on retail investors.[4] There was one exception where Hunsader's thesis might hold true. An HFT firm could route an order to one of the few dark pools that rely on the consolidated tape for pricing, hoping to be executed at a stale price.

Hunsader also had suggested that HFT firms had deliberately slowed the consolidated tape on May 6, just before the Flash Crash, roiling pricing information and thus precipitating the selloff. The regulators found no direct evidence of this at all. But they did not rule out that traders might be deliberately slowing the data on other days, and they said they intended to look into the possibility. As a result, on November 3, 2010, the SEC voted unanimously to prohibit brokers from providing customers with "naked sponsored access," or a direct, unsupervised connection to an exchange. The SEC wanted to eliminate the possibility that some high-frequency traders were not playing by the rules. Customers of the brokers would now have to be subject to the brokers' supervision and risk management controls.

SEC Chairman Schapiro likened naked access to lending a car to an unlicensed driver. "This rule," she said, "requires that the broker-dealers not only remain in the car but also maintain control of it so we can all be assured that the rules of the road will be observed before the car is put into drive."

One glaring omission in the joint report was an examination of the structure that the market played in allowing the Flash Crash to occur. After all, this was the market built by the SEC, supposedly modeled on Congress's 1975 decree. The market was supposed to be fair efficient, and friendly to long-term investors. And it turned out that it wasn't any of these things. Because of the micro-managing of the SEC, the market had become unnecessarily complicated, disproportionately volatile, and less accountable than ever before. The old system that had been dominated by human market makers may have been imperfect, but it had worked fairly well for decades. The new market had broken down in less than 3 years. The Congress and the regulators' biggest "success" was driving out most of the human market makers and replacing them with machines. But they managed to drive out most of the human investors, too, engendering a huge outflow of capital when America's struggling companies most needed it.

Endnotes

1. See Chapter 9, "The Trouble with Mary—and Gary."

2. E-mail from Nagy to author, October 6, 2010.

3. Report of the staffs of the CFTC and SEC to the Joint Advisory Committee on Emerging Issues, "Findings Regarding the Market Events of May 6, 2010," 64–65.

4. "Findings," 78.

24

Investing in a Shark-Infested Market

As harrowing a place as the stock market is today, Scottish transplant Jim McCaughan believes it represents a great opportunity for long-term investors with stomachs of iron and nerves of steel.

"The returns on the underlying capital are very high," he argues. Of course, investors must screw up their courage because a market dominated by the high-frequency trading (HFT) firms looks very dangerous. McCaughan recommends that investors commit to the market long term and ignore as best they can the wild, short-term price swings.

McCaughan is the CEO of Principal Global Investors, which manages $212 billion in assets, including those held by 12 of the 25 largest U.S. pension funds. He understands the retail investors' reason for disengaging from the market; nevertheless, he believes the move to be unwise. Someday, McCaughan says, most of the volatility will go away, and stocks once again will be in great demand.

The process might take five to ten years, which is why he counsels a long-term horizon. In part, the diminution in volatility will be a consequence of improved economic conditions; and in part it will stem from regulatory changes aimed at dampening the wild market swings that today seem commonplace.

He believes that the agency also would re-establish the uptick rule, which once made it more difficult to sell stocks short in a rapidly declining market.[1]

McCaughan says investing in today's climate requires a disciplined rebalancing of one's portfolio to reflect one's investment goals, risk profile, and financial needs. Older persons nearing retirement, for instance, would want to decrease their equity holdings and increase their holdings of safer investment instruments such as high-grade bonds.

"If you are a do-it-yourself investor, it means refusing to chase prices—waiting for bad days in the market to buy," he says.

For those investors who'd rather have a professional handle their portfolios, McCaughan recommends *life-cycle funds*, also known in some quarters as *target date* funds. These are an increasingly popular way to save for retirement. The funds have a term based on the investor's expected date of retirement. For younger investors with a time horizon of ten or more years, the bias now is on equities. The bias switches toward less risky fixed-income investments as the target date draws near.

The funds invest in domestic and foreign equities and real estate.

McCaughan adds that if you hope to retire in, say, 5 years but expect to hang around for another 20 or so years, equities also should be part of your portfolio.

David Hartzell, the CEO of Cornell Capital Management in Buffalo, New York, recommends a strategy called *dividend capture*, which was pioneered by Japanese insurance companies. He cites four ways in which individuals can use dividend capture to decrease volatility in their portfolio and increase cash flow by buying and selling stocks that pay a dividend of 5% or more.

In the first case, an investor buys the stock two weeks before it goes ex-dividend and then sells the stock two days prior to the ex-dividend date. The person who owns the stock on the ex-dividend date receives the dividend. The stock generally decreases in value afterward by the amount of the dividend. Hartzell said this strategy works because of abnormal volume and a rise in a stock's price immediately prior to the ex-dividend date. In the second instance, an investor buys the stock the day before the ex-dividend date, captures the dividend, and then sells it the following day. In a rising market, this is the simplest, most efficient, and least volatile way to capture dividends, he says. A third strategy is to buy the stock after the ex-dividend date and hold on to it until the payment date, the day the dividend check is actually paid out by the company. Excess returns are relatively high on the payment date and on several trading days immediately after it, Hartzell says. The fourth strategy is to short the stock after it goes ex-dividend and then cover the short sale within seven days to take advantage of the drop in price after the stock goes ex-dividend. In 2004, Hartzell wrote a book on the topic with Mohammed Sorathia titled *Dividend Capture: From Theory to Practical Application*.

Investors might be tempted to invest in options to take advantage of wild market gyrations or to hedge their stocks with these instruments. This is not a great idea for average investors, says Bradley Kay, director of European ETF research for Morningstar, the investment research company.

"They are more of a hassle than they are worth," says Kay. Furthermore, professionals who must use these instruments to hedge their portfolios have driven up their costs to high levels.

Kay recommends that individual investors make certain that the duration of assets in their portfolios is matched to expected liabilities. For example, you don't want to be in long-term investments if you have a big expense looming. Furthermore, investors should appreciate that money in the market is money at risk. Money needed for medical expenses, or as a cushion against possible job loss, should not be in the stock market, he says. And if you are investing in bond funds in this volatile period, the average duration of the fund's portfolio should not be longer than four to five years.

Stock investing in the short-run is risky, Kay says, because of the sharp, violent swings caused by HFT and due to the movements of exchange-traded funds (ETFs), which will cause the underlying securities held by these funds to bounce around quite a bit. But, like McCaughan, Kay believes that the short-term swings will not injure long-term investors who buy and hold stocks for five years or longer.

Gary Gastineau, a principal at ETF Consultants, Summit, New Jersey, recommends long-term investments in ETFs. He believes that the circuit breakers instituted by the Securities and Exchange Commission (SEC) and the Commodities Futures Trading Commission (CFTC) will protect investors from rapid declines due to correlation.

Gastineau argues that ETFs are superior to mutual funds because their operating expenses are considerably lower. Everyone in a mutual fund pays a cost for everyone else in the fund being invested, and everyone pays a cost for anyone leaving the fund. On average, he says, this charge amounts to half a percent every year. In an ETF, the individual pays a commission going in and out but is not penalized by other investors going in and out of the safe ETF. So right off the bat, he says, an ETF has a half of a percent annual advantage over traditional mutual funds.

My own solution is to wait for days when the major indexes are falling and purchase low-cap and mid-cap stocks with strong earnings, healthy cash flow, and a decent dividend—and which trade at wide spreads because of low trading volumes. The dividend at least should be higher than the rate on a 5-year CD. I generally buy these investments in my tax-free retirement account.

Academic studies have shown that low-cap stocks outperform most other stocks over the long term. And because they are not among the 1,500 largest capitalization stocks, they hold less interest for high-frequency traders.

I purchase such stocks at prices close to the bid—and sometimes at prices below the bid on an especially volatile day. I never, ever use a market order because that guarantees that I will pay the full spread. Only suckers and people who can't afford to wait to make a buy or a sell use market orders.

Before I buy a low-cap or mid-cap mutual fund, I take the top three holdings of the funds and screen them to make sure they are not overpriced or underperforming. If any of those top three stocks does not pass the earnings and cash flow and dividend test, I don't buy the fund. I assume that the fund's manager doesn't know what he's doing.

I also set a profit target for each stock that I buy for the next 12 months. If it reaches that objective early for no fundamental reason, I sell it and establish a new downside target at which to buy it back again at a later date. My intention is to hold a good company for the long term but to take my money and run if it becomes overpriced in the near term. I am limited by my company's ethics, which require me to hold a stock a minimum of three months and prohibit short sales and speculating with options.

One final rule that I follow: I never buy in the morning or sell in the afternoon. Retail investors tend to be active first thing in the morning, and professionals are out in force to scalp them. Because they submit so many market orders, it's a good time to sell. Prices settle down in the afternoon as professional traders take over and narrow the spreads, which makes it a better time to buy.

I use research tools. I use my own publication, *Barron's*, as a starting point for many investments. *The Wall Street Journal, The Economist, Financial Times*, Bloomberg, Market Watch, and Reuters all are credible daily sources of investment news.

Investment publications that have staffs of veteran, hard-charging, highly curious journalists can provide an excellent starting point for an investor and keep investors apprised of what is going on in the market as a whole and in particular sectors and companies. "Buy and hold" doesn't mean "buy and forget." Investors must be constantly vigilant of the economic environment and the prospects for the companies in their portfolios.

The blogs of professional investors and economists also can be important sources of information to help you shape your view of the markets. Barry Ritholtz's "Big Picture" blog has excellent discussions about the broad economy. Ed Yardeni's subscription newsletter is another excellent read. Asset manager John Maulden's "Outside the Box" is a fine site for investors seeking contrarian viewpoints. Investors should go to the Web site of Cumberland Advisors and sign up at no charge for David Kotok's market musings. PNC chief economist Stuart Hoffman is regularly prescient, and his reports are available free-of-charge on the banking company's Web site. William Dunkelberg's analysis of small business conditions is an important market bellwether. He posts his analysis on the site of the National Federation of Independent Business. And the Association of American Railroads posts to the Web on a monthly basis its "Rail Time Indicators" report, which is perused by Buffet and Alan Greenspan and other financial experts for clues about the direction of the economy.

Yahoo! Finance lists the star analysts for each company. I use a service that gives me access to their research.

In addition to important news, both *Barron's* and *The Wall Street Journal* have excellent online tools to aid investors in conducting their fundamental research, like a basic version of StockGrader. The major stock and commodities exchanges also provide useful data and educational material.

Investing is hard work. Warren Buffet did not become the world's most successful investor by relying on the representations of others. I recommend that investors studiously review a company's SEC filings, which are available online at the agency's Web site. And before investing, an investor should know what the short interest is in a stock; what the spread in its bid and asked price in the stock has been for the past year; analysts' expectations for earnings; and similar information for other stocks in the same sector.

But there is no sure-fire method for a retail investor to beat the market. It has become a shark tank, and we are the anchovies. Every time you buy or sell a stock, you are rolling the dice and hoping for a good outcome.

Endnotes

1. Report of the staffs of the CFTC and SEC to the Joint Advisory Committee on Emerging Regulatory Issues, "Preliminary Findings Regarding the Market Events of May 6, 2010." Washington, DC (2010): 28–30.

INDEX

FINANCIAL TIMES

In an increasingly competitive world, it is quality
of thinking that gives an edge—an idea that opens new
doors, a technique that solves a problem, or an insight
that simply helps make sense of it all.

We work with leading authors in the various arenas
of business and finance to bring cutting-edge thinking
and best-learning practices to a global market.

It is our goal to create world-class print publications
and electronic products that give readers
knowledge and understanding that can then be
applied, whether studying or at work.

To find out more about our business
products, you can visit us at www.ftpress.com.